GATS.

A Guide to Junior Push In – Pop Out Airguns.

This first edition of GATS was written and composed using a Packard Bell Easynote TX86 laptop with Windows 7, Word and Excel programmes.

All photographs were taken by the Author using a Canon EOS 500D camera fitted with either a Canon EF-S IS 18-55mm or EF 50mm f/2.5 Macro lens.

Sue Willcox

An absolute gem, who is patient enough to endure all of my junk and clutter.

I would welcome any comments, observations and information about gats or their accessories and invite readers to e mail me at the following address.

malcolmatk@aol.com.

Contents.

Acknowledgments.

My thanks go to all the people who have helped with information, advice and for letting me examine items from their collections, to the auction houses and the dealers at the arms fairs, details of which can be found in the where to buy section. To all my numerous shooting friends, especially Stevie Vranch, Robert Morgan, Paul Chambers, John Lay, Alan Harvey and the late and very sadly missed Eric Dougliss, who was one of the best ambassadors ever for all aspects of the shooting sports.

My special thanks go to Robert Morgan for his efforts in proofreading the entire manuscript and also being able to prove that my spellchecker was dyslexic.

Introduction.

Anyone interested in airguns or connected with shooting, collecting or dealing with militaria will know of the push in, pop out type air pistols generically known as gats, in many ways one of the most ignored of all the collectable airguns.

One of the main aims of this book is to try to establish a reasonably creditable dating line for the various makes, which somewhat to my surprise turned out to be far more numerous than at first imagined. Even common versions show surprising variations and what was at first thought to be a fairly simple project soon proved that there was still much to learn.

In researching this book many varied and differing opinions were found regarding dating and the actual manufacturers. Where there is a lack of detailed information the best available but possibly unsubstantiated ideas will be included, hopefully the majority of details given will be correct but anything incorrect is my fault and I would be more than happy for anyone who can supply updated or corrected details to contact me. Spaces will be left in various sections for notes and other details obtained after the main section was written.

On the subject of the names for this type of pistol, there have been quite a few interesting variations but I had settled on push in, pop out pistols or PIPOP's but on further consideration decided to go for gat, this being the most common generic title in Great Britain of this type of pistol.

The majority of pistols covered in this book can trace their ancestry back to American H.M.Quackenbush's many patents and his various modifications of other peoples pistols, a patent of 1876 covered a concentric barrel pistol that was cocked by pushing in, then pulling out the barrel, but the important one with all the attributes of a gat was American patent no.188028 of 1877 which covered a push in pop out concentric barrel pistol with the spring exposed on the forward part of the barrel. Searching through the British Patent Office Abridgment of Patents for pneumatic weapons has so far drawn a blank for a British version of this patent but it is possible that it might just be found under toy patents as air pistols were sometimes classed as such.

Having had such a promising start in America the gat type was soon superseded by other pistol patterns and apart from some lighter type junior rifles with push in pull out systems (Quakenbush No.1 rifle and others) did not appear to take to the gat type pistol with any great enthusiasm.

Other 19th century countries with little or no interest in the gat type pistol included France, and Belgium, but as both of these had thriving industries producing Flobert, Velodog and other cheap pistols and rifles in vast quantities with little or no legislation to hamper ownership, there appeared to be little interest in cheap air weapons generally. A few items from these countries can be found but nothing like the vast numbers produced in Britain and Germany.

Both Britain and Germany were producing huge quantities of small arms during the 19th and early 20th centuries, but Britain was concentrating on Empire building and the consequent military arms race, plus selling weapons of all qualities worldwide. It took the debacle of the Boer War to wake the British people up to the appalling fact that the British Army was being outshot, this lead to a rise in interest in target shooting and pistol practice. However subsequent legislation in this crowded island managed to stifle the use of firearms but consequently increased the interest and production of air weapons, so British airgun production really started to take off between the Boer and 1st World War, production was mostly confined to air rifles but a few of the rarer air pistols did emerge during this period.

Germany and the associated Germanic countries had a widespread and historic arms manufacturing industry and took an early lead in gat production starting with cast iron pistols which later became the Dolla and various other types in the 1880's, those and other air rifles were produced in huge quantities and sold at such cheap prices that it was probably not worthwhile to try to manufacture them elsewhere as it was much easier to buy them in. Early British catalogues show at least five or six different models with a wide variety of finishes and prices, some claiming to be British made or with a British name, a fact that should be taken with a huge pinch of salt as advertising of the period was about as accurate as a chocolate watch!. Most if not all were of distinctly Germanic appearance or manufacture.

At the end of both the 1st and 2nd World Wars German arms production was decimated, however airgun production was resumed quite quickly after both wars, but war reparations meant firms were sometimes badly effected and lost production facilities, manufacturing rights and titles or after WW2 were dismantled and absorbed into the Allied or Soviet spheres of influence.

Conventions.

Catalogues. Much of the study of early pistols involves searching through 19th and early 20th century catalogues, however there are some actual problems associated with this. Having been in the printing trade in the mid 1960's I ended up as a journeyman hand compositor just as film setting wiped out traditional hand and metal typesetting. I am fully aware that in the era of woodcuts, copper engraving, electrotyping and photogravure many of the printing blocks were used for years as they were a significant cost item, usually only replaced when worn out, I spotted an excellent example in one catalogue where a Dare Devil Dinkum which is a butt cylinder pistol cocked via a pull down cocking rod using a special tool much like the later Diana Model 1 tinplate had the cocking knob missing from beneath the butt, at first glance it represented a totally unknown pistol but was due entirely to a damaged plate. Also, just as some product descriptions were almost but not quite exactly true, it was not unknown for blocks of one pistol to be reused in the cheaper catalogues for an entirely different item; some catalogues even claimed that they were the makers of different air weapons and spuriously applied their names to them.

Pistols. When described in text a lower case 'g' was used when referring to generic gat type pistols, with an upper case 'G' used when referring to Harrington Gat pistols only.

Types. Each major group of pistols has a dedicated section, minor or unknown makes may be combined into a group section, but rarer pistols have their own individual sections.

Pistol Numbering. The majority of the pistols pictured in this book have a number attached, i.e. Pistol no. 51. This is a numbering system for items from my own collection, which uses tie on or white sticky labels and became a useful way of linking pictures to the text. Where no number appears these may be pictures obtained from pistols seen elsewhere, but if they come from other collections an acknowledgment will appear, usually in the text or beneath the picture itself.

Values. A price range will be shown first giving an estimated or known purchase price in today's market, allowing that prices for some pistols seem to have risen quite sharply since 2005. Following that will be a list of prices obtained at auction since 2000, there is a wide variation shown but as the price obtained depends on a great deal on condition and if the lots contain large mixed quantities and types of pistols then rarer items can sometimes be purchased quite cheaply. One thing to remember is that the auction prices shown are the bid price and these are subject to buyer's premium, VAT on the premium, credit card and delivery charges, these can add an additional 20 to 30% to the price, so suggest adding 25% to the auction prices shown to obtain a more realistic price.

Pricing. British currency appearing in catalogues is divided into pre-decimal and decimal currency, the designation of the coinage was similar but the actual values changed considerably.

Pre-decimal coinage apart from the higher value notes consisted of a pound (£) divided into 20 shillings (s. or /-) or 240 pennies (d.) in a variety of different value combinations. Replaced by decimal coinage in 1968 – 69, which used the same pound (£) but now divided into 100 pence (p).

Pre-decimal.		Common nicknames.	Decimal value.
1 Pound	(£1).	Pound, Quid or Nicker.	£1
10 shillings	(10/-)	10 Bob	50p
5 shillings	(5/-)	Crown or Dollar (rare in normal use)	25p
2 shillings & 6 pence		Half a Crown or Half a Dollar	12 1/2p
2 shillings	(2/-)	2 Bob or a Florin	10p
1 shilling	(1/-)	Bob	5p
Sixpence	(6d)	Tanner	2 1/2p
Threepence	(3d)	Joey (silver) Thrupenny Bit (brass)	1 1/4p
Penny	(1d)	Copper	~ 4/10p

Also both pre and post decimal coinage included half pennies but with rising prices the decimal one was found to be of little value considering the amount of metal in circulation and was soon discontinued. Although decimal coinage has been in use for over forty years it is somewhat indicative of public feeling that none of the replacement coinage has ever gained a popular nickname.

Measurements. Dimensions and weights are shown in both Imperial and Metric measurements. Depending on how the Imperial measurements were taken the results are either shown as fractions (ruler) or in 100ths (calliper). Where possible the pistols were measured using a vertical vernier calliper with the sights aligned with the calliper upright and the tip of the butt on the baseplate to give an un-cocked overall length. Weights were obtained using Salter mechanical and electronic Max View scales.

The only other odd measurement is grains, (not to be confused with grams) which is a measure restricted to measuring weights of projectiles and propellants. It consists of 7000 grains (grs) per pound (lb). Used in this book for weights of pellets used for the chronograph velocity tests. Those weights were obtained by weighing a random selection of ten pellets from a tin and dividing by ten to give an average weight per pellet.

Chronograph Testing. Was undertaken using a Shooting Crony type F1 chronograph with the addition of an L.E.D. diffuser lighting set. Ten results were obtained for each gun tested and entered into an Excel spread-sheet, these results were then averaged to give velocity reading in feet per second (fps).

To convert the fps results into foot/pounds (ft/lbs) the Crony formula was used.

Average velocity x ave. vel. x pellet weight in grains divided by 450240 = ft/lbs

i.e. 416.03 fps x 416.03 fps x 7.16 grains divided by 450240 = 2.75 ft/lbs.

When testing it was thought appropriate to use standard diabalo style pellets of reasonable quality rather than better quality target type flatheads as those pellets were not available when the majority of these pistols were in use. In most cases people brought the cheapest pellet available as the inaccuracy of gats did not warrant spending hard earned pocket money on better projectiles. This did however cause a few problems when using the chronograph as the pellets chosen showed marked differences in diameter when placed in the pistols, in fact some pellets were so loose that they actually dropped straight through the barrel, this and the inherent inaccuracy gave rise to spurious readings by not consistently passing over the detectors, this was addressed by ignoring the loose pellets results and using a target behind the chronograph to eliminate spurious results from wayward shots. The final results were somewhat of a surprise especially when converted to foot pounds as even pistols thought to be extra powerful turned out to be nowhere near the British limit of six foot pounds.

Searching for gats.

It used to be possible to find gats in all manner of places but with increased legislation many of the traditional hunting grounds have ceased trading in airguns and no longer keep them in stock. Having said that, airguns do occasionally turn up at car boot sales, charity shops, antique shops and also toy fairs but it's probably much better to try some of the following places.

Arms Fairs, Auctions, Dealers, Gun Shops, Adverts, Friends and Relations.

Arms Fairs. These are held all over the country, details and dates can usually be found in the shooting press. Not normally dedicated to airguns but most will have airgun dealers who regularly attend these shows, plus there is always a treasure house of other things to see. My favourites include Birmingham and Bisley, its rare not to unearth several items of interest at these two shows.

Auctions. Most auction houses which hold dedicated arms or militaria sales appear to be taking increasing amounts of airguns, possibly customers are starting to realise the values of the rarer airguns are increasing but have not yet hit the high prices of normal weapons. Whatever the reason, there are opportunities for the knowledgeable to purchase bargains and sometimes real rarities can be found in job lots of little apparent value. If possible, view before the sale but if that's not possible you can always place absentee or postal bids, remembering that premium and other charges have to be added. It's most important to always read the terms and conditions in the catalogue and fully read the descriptions of the items including any of the cryptic abbreviations.

Apart from local general auctions, I normally use two dedicated auction houses.

Holt's. Auctioneers of fine modern and antique guns. A really friendly and helpful firm based in Norfolk, their sales are divided into two parts, the main and sealed bid sections. When sales occur, both parts can be viewed at Princess Louise House, Hammersmith where the main sale is held, it is followed a few days later by the sealed bid sale which takes place in Norfolk.

Wallis and Wallis. Long established auctioneers of Lewes in East Sussex who hold several sales per year of militaria, arms and armour, they also hold separate sales of toys. Of especial interest are the Connoisseur Collectors sales catalogues which contain some magnificent items of militaria and weaponry.

Dealers. My favourite dealers at the arms fairs are all genuine characters and are always ready with a joke, most of them have knowledge and collections that far exceed my puny efforts. In no particular order they are Conor with his airgun stand, my good friend Alan Harvey who let me examine several rare items for inclusion in the book, Keith Bayliss (R L Gun Co.) with a brilliant selection of rare guns on his table and Henry Krank and Company Limited of Pudsey, West Yorkshire with a good selection of airguns on the website and in the specialised catalogue. Other dealers can be found in the shooting magazines but changes in the law have stopped direct mail order unless it goes Registered Firearms Dealers (RFD), which is a bit of an inconvenience to say the least.

Gun Shops. Always worth getting to know the staff at your local gun-shop, I spent many a Saturday of my misspent youth hanging around and helping in the local shop and picked up plenty of valuable knowledge. Let them know what you are collecting and with the wide circle of customers they have, you may well turn up a real treasure.

Adverts. If found in the shooting press the details were mostly dealt with in the Dealers section, however it is still possible to find adverts in local shop windows, in country editions of the local free papers and the trading papers.

Friends and Relations. Well, this can really be a fruitful area to explore especially if there are shooting members amongst friends or relations, I have truly lost count of the number of older people who on finding out I was preparing this book informed me they owned and had great fun with a gat of some type during their childhood. Occasionally they do manage to turn one up from its slumbers buried in the attic or shed. Word of mouth can also reap surprising dividends as sometimes a real rarity or even a carrier bagful of bits and pieces can turn up completely out of the blue.

Condition. When buying gats it's rare to find broken ones, occasionally they fail to cock, sometimes the pellet push pin is missing, in most cases unless the pistol in question is extremely rare, leave it alone as a better version is bound to appear later. Always go for the best condition you can afford as gats were cheap and used hard with little or no maintenance, in consequence finish suffered accordingly. Mint, boxed gats will always attract a premium and will retain or even increase their value in later years. In contrast tatty pistols will always remain at the lower end of the market.

Early pistols.

The earliest versions of what later turned out to be the gat type pistol appear to have originated in America during the latter part of the 19th century and were inventions and modifications from the fertile brain of H.M.Quackenbush, who was involved with several pistols including one cocked by pushing down a vertical rod in the grip, one cocked by pulling down a rod to cock a piston in the butt in a similar manner to a Diana tinplate Model 1, another version cocked by pulling out the barrel, yet another by pushing it in and pulling it out and eventually in 1877 a gat like pistol. The push/pull system was very successful in Quackenbush no. 1 and no. 7 air rifles, but most pistols appear to have been produced or possibly improved by other people such as Haviland and Gunn, Bedford, Walker, Pope plus others who all helped with the development of the various improvements. Early pistols directly attributed to Quackenbush are very thin on the ground, in fact they are as rare as a live dodo, but the slightly later American pistols can be found albeit at a cost as they are still counted as being amongst the rocking horse droppings area of air pistol collecting.

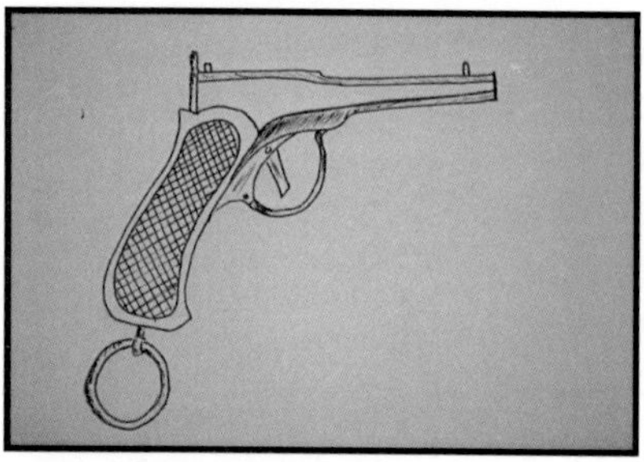

Sketch of 1872 Haviland & Gunn.

Sketch of 1877 Quackenbush Mod.1.

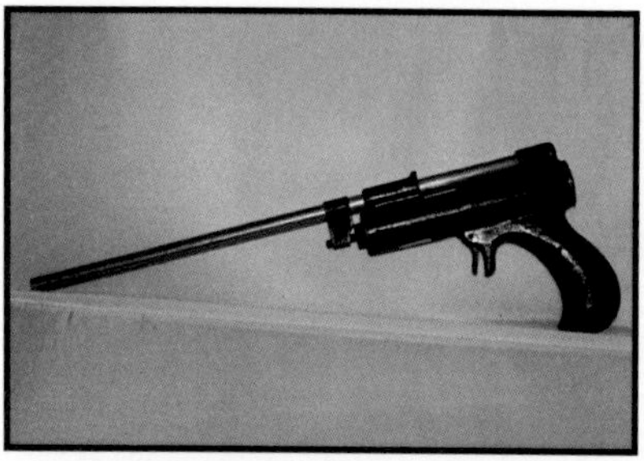

Pistol no. 70, Pope Brothers, closed.

Opened to cock pistol and load pellet.

End cap of Pope with patents.

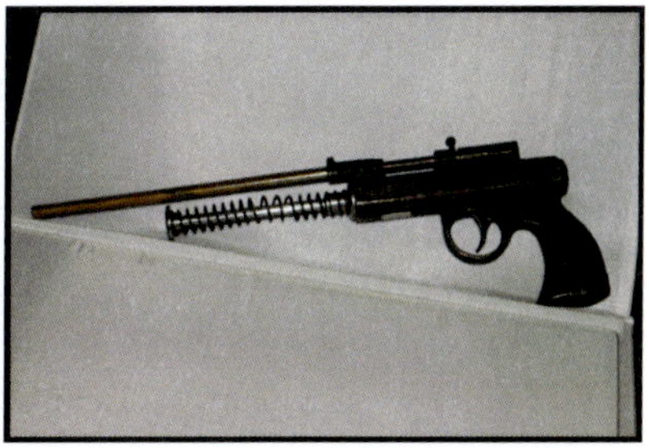

Pistol no. 69, Bedford & Walker.

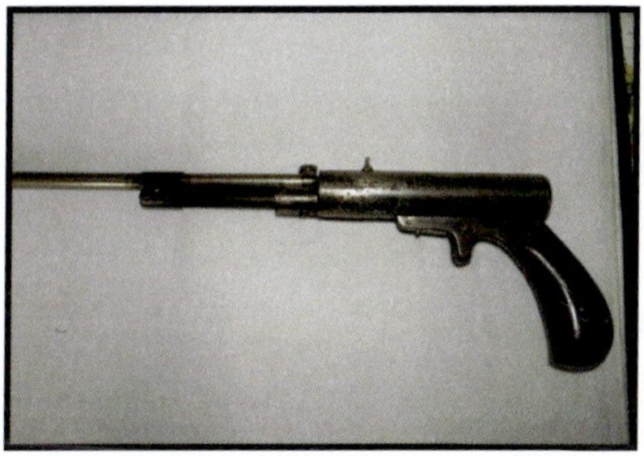

Pistol no.65, Champion closed.

Open and barrel rod pushed in to cock.

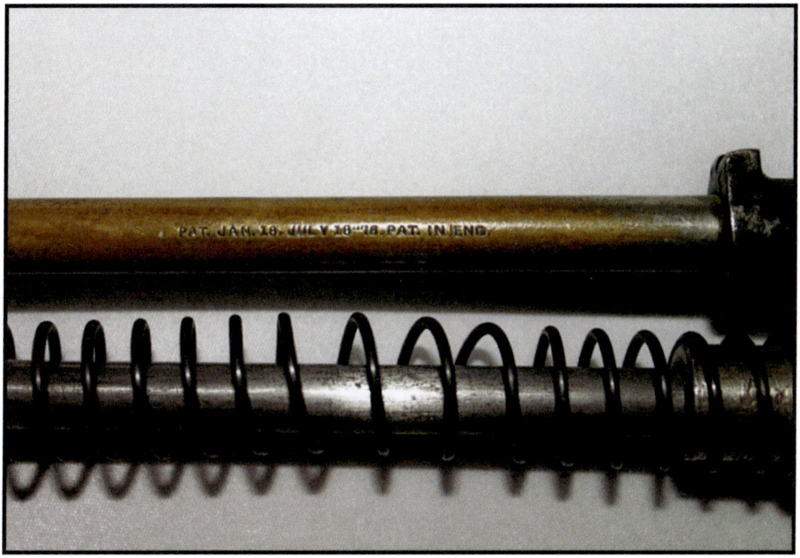

Pistol no.69, Bedford & Walker, patent details on left side of barrel.

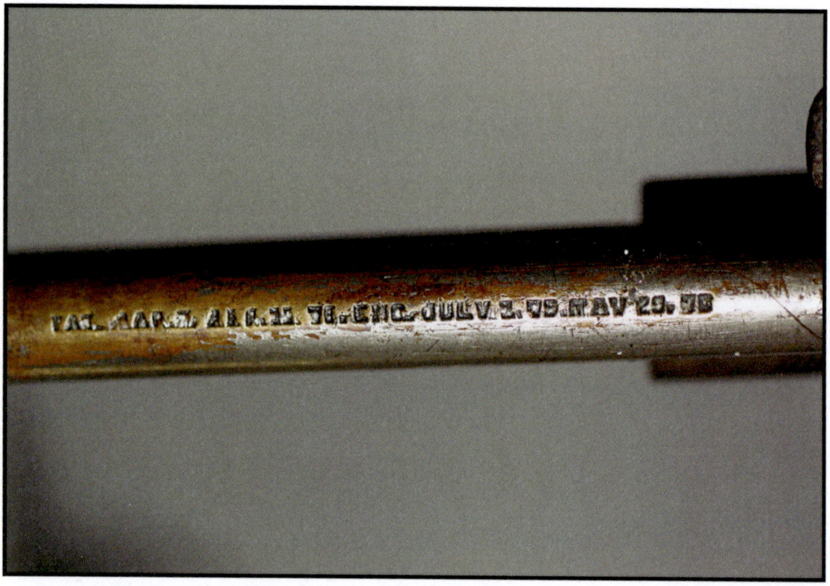

Pistol no.65, Iver Johnston, Champion, patent numbers on top of barrel.

Descriptions and Dimensions.

Sketch of Havilland and Gunn pistol, produced in1872 with pull down cocking using attached pull ring, cylinder in butt, breech closure by swinging plate, this pistol was unsuccessful and very short lived, probably due to the heavy rod and ring shooting back into the butt also the breech sealing lacked a pellet pushing system and was not very efficient. However later German pistols were very closly related to this pistol, albeit most with separate cocking tools to reduce the weight of the rebounding cocking rod and much improved breech systems.

Sketch of the 1877 Quackenbush, the very simplicity of this pistol is an example of least is more. OK, it was never going to be a target quality weapon but as a fun knockabout pistol it really has stood the test of time as modified versions are still being produced over one hundred and thirty years later. Of note is the apparent similarity between the body castings of the Pope and the Champion and the Model 1 Quackenbush pistols. In fact on both of those pistols if the cocking rod was replaced by a barrel and return spring they would with very few other alterations become viable versions of a gat.

Pistol no. 70, cast iron, black enamelled frame and nickelled barrel Pope rifle air pistol, operated by pulling out brass barrel to cock the action, while open a pellet or dart is inserted and barrel pushed back into battery. The pistol is now ready to fire, unfortunately this pistol was fitted with 1¾ springs and was coilbound and not cocking, removing excess spring made it work but exceedingly feeble. Hole in butt for wire shoulder stock. Circa 1875, original Quackenbush American patent 156809. British patents 1391 & 1392 appear in 1876 issued to A.A.Pope (A.C.Carcey) on 30th March.

Overall length. 12 1/4'' 308mm. Weight. 1lb 4 1/4 oz 573 grm.

Pistol no. 69, cast iron Bedford and Walker may also be known as the Eureka, another design owing it's origins to Quackenbush, it was modified according to an American patent no. 172376 issued on 18th January 1876 to Bedford but the more important American patent no. 179984 was issued to George Walker on 18th July 1876, which covered the bolt operated breech with pusher pin, a feature still in use on lots of modern air and CO^2 weapons. English patent no.23 was issued on January 3rd 1876 to A.O.Surett, H.N.Sheldon & J.R.M.Squire (A.Bedford). Cocked by pushing in the spring loaded rod under the brass barrel, which automatically returns when released, loaded by using the bolt action. Black painted finish with nickelled fittings, this pistol has been fitted with a replacement pusher knob and a return spring which should be of smaller diameter.

Overall length. 13 1/8'' 347mm. Weight. 1lb 14 1/4 oz 859 grm.

Pistol no. 65, cast iron Champion air pistol, possibly made by several firms including Iver Johnson Arms & Cycle Works, Worcester, Massachusetts. Dated at around 1878 as patent dates 1871 to 1876 on barrel. English patent no. 2257 issued on May 29th 1876, to W.R.Lake (I.Johnson & M.Bye). Pistols were available in blue, nickel and later as per this pistol in a deluxe version with nickel finish and rosewood grips. To operate the barrel is unlatched and dropped 90 degrees to form a tee handle which is pushed in to cock action, pellet is then placed in barrel which is pulled out, rotated back into battery and locked with clever rotary breech seal like a miniature version of the Webley Mark II Service Rifle. Also advertised as a cheaper version called the Victor.

Overall length. 14 5/16'' 377mm. Weight. 1lb 3 7/8 oz 564 grm.

Values.

All of the above £100 to £450+ dependant on condition. Except for the H & G and the Quackenbush Model 1 pistols which are extremely rare and expensive.

Auction.

Pope, £400 (boxed), £85, £70, £60, £20 & £90.

Bedford & Walker, £100 & £130.

Champion, £240.

Quackenbush No. 1 air rifle, £180, £300 & £170.

Notes.

Anson Firefly.

The Firefly was manufactured by E. Anson, Steelhouse Lane, Birmingham.

A rare and distinct design which is probably one of the ugliest of all the gats, uncomfortable to hold and although it has a very short barrel travel it is fitted with a double spring which makes it difficult to cock, these faults probably deterred any child from using it, advertised around 1932 to 33, it probably hung on into the late 30's but the obvious rarity would seem to point to limited sales.

Pistol no.29, right side view showing cast frame and grip.

Markings, Right side.

Left side.

Pistol no.29, left side showing the rear sight which is bent up out of cylinder

This pistol is unusual in that the spring slider is black painted wood, (which probably broke up with use) also it is fitted with a keeper spring for the pusher pin which is usually missing. Standard finish was black enamel with a nickel plated chamber. Sights consist of a small screw in rounded bead foresight and a V notch bent up from the body of the cylinder at the rear. Note the cut out in the trigger to clear one of the frame securing nuts.

Dimensions.

Overall length. 6 15/16'' 177mm. Weight. 1lb 0 3/8 oz 454 grm.

Values.

As much as you want to pay for a very rare pistol, if very lucky around £175 to £400 for a clean example, but expect to pay more and considerably more for a mint boxed version with all the bits. Note, prices are rising sharply in 2011.

Auction. £40, £100. plus several others did not reach their reserve prices.

Mid. 2011 auction estimates have risen very quickly up to £500 to £700.

Barnett Nitro 45 Pistol.

This pistol appeared in the 1990's and was made by Barnett, a company more usually known for their most excellent and innovative crossbow designs.

The pistol packaging lists Barnett as either the UK, Canada, Florida or France although the pistol itself is marked Made in England, this could mean that the pistol was manufactured in the other countries or it is more probable that the addresses in the other countries were acting as distributors.

Whatever the case this is a large and handy pistol, mostly manufactured using what appears to be injection moulded polymer or resin reinforced plastic, the design probably represents the high point of gat development, the large grips and squared barrel shroud go some way toward eliminating the barrel jump problem endemic with this type of pistol. Overall a very nice design, not known if the production continued past 2000, as have not seen any new stock on sale since that time. Calibre is .177, not known if a .22 version was produced.

An unpackaged pistol was seen, but the only difference was the use of a brass muzzle nut which may mean that it was made slightly earlier than no. 56.

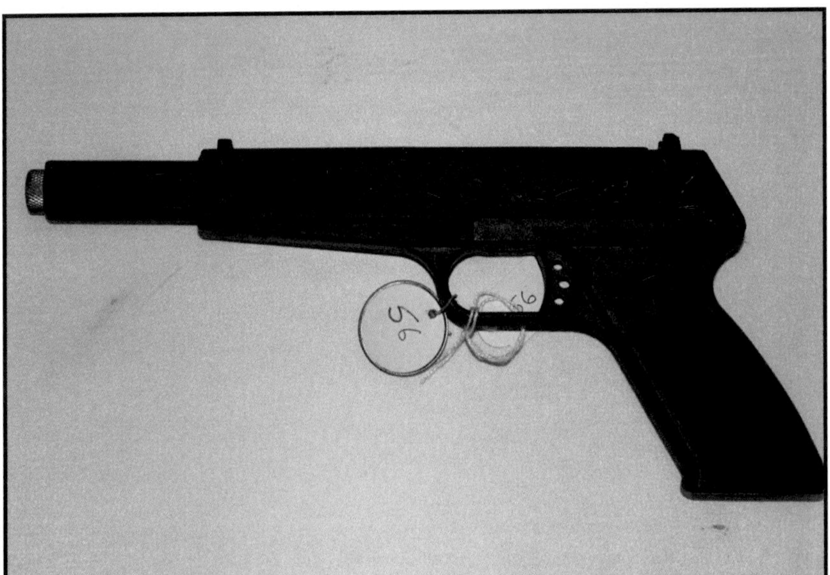

Pistol no. 56, left side view, note alloy muzzle nut.

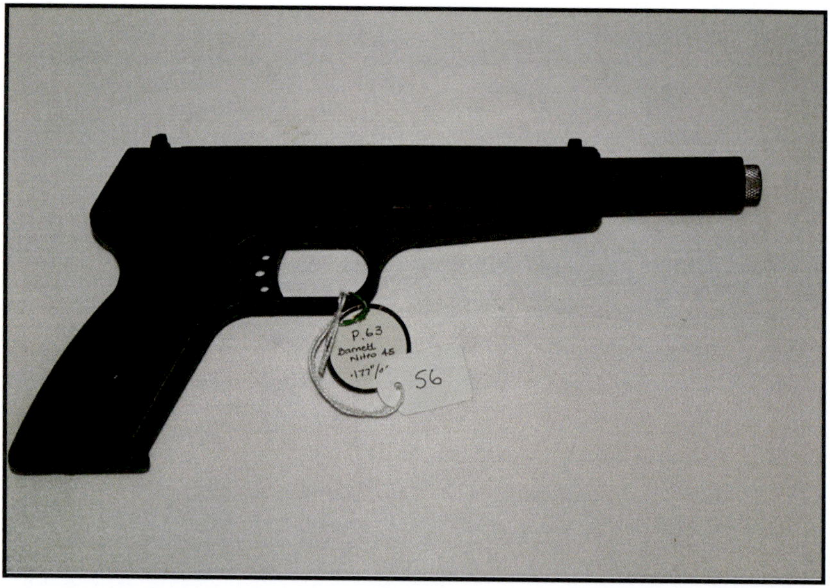

Pistol no. 56, right side view, note, circular P63 tag from a previous collection.

Pistol no. 56, right side view, note detail of trademark and safety catch.

Pistol no. 56, left side view, note detail of calibre, low power mark and safety.

Pistol no. 56, in moulded clamshell package, has 6 darts but pellet pack missing.

Pistol no. 56, rear of clamshell package, showing instructions and addresses.

Advertised in Guns Review in November 1993 and August 1994 as the new Nitro Pistol, available from Dept. GR Barnett, Dock Meadow Drive, Lansfield, Wolverhampton, West Midlands, WV4 6UD.

Dimensions.

Overall length. 13 1/2" 265mm. Weight. 11 1/16 oz 282 grm.

Values.

Brought as part of a collection, estimate £25 to £40.

Auction. None seen as single lots.

Britannia Pistols

Again one of those pistols with an as yet unknown maker, the box art and the pistols are marked British Made and Made in England respectively and as there are no apparent Germanic equivalent it is probably fair to assume this actually is an English pistol. Surprisingly both pistols examined were boxed and although the chromed pistol box was in poor order the drawings on the labels of both boxes bear little resemblance to the actual pistols enclosed, in fact they resemble early Britons or possibly a Scout with a trigger guard, it may even be possible that there was an earlier and somewhat different version of this pistol.

The pistols are constructed of heavy steel tubing and substantial steel pressings and are generally well made although some details of construction involve brazing which is quite frankly of mediocre quality. Available in blue or chrome finish and supplied boxed with a box of pellets and a paper pack of darts. Estimated date of around the 1930's, as for the maker, C.G.Bonehill of Birmingham produced an air rifle called the Britannia just before WW1, however this may prove to be one of those coincidences, as there is no evidence that Bonehill had anything at all to do with the production of these pistols.

Pistol no.13, right side, note un-plated steel trigger and blued front post sight .

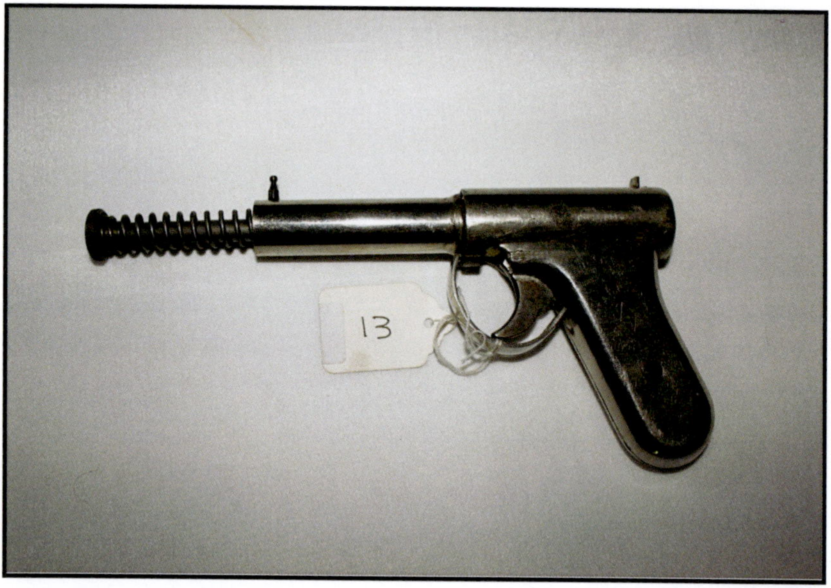

Pistol no.13, left side.

Pistol no.13, box lid unfortunately somewhat worn.

Pistol no.13, inside box, note pellet or dart pack retaining box on right.

Pistol no.13, trademark on right grip, note the crude screws.

Pistol no.13, note Made in England stamping around diamond trademark.

Pistol no.27, seems to be better made than no.13, note fitted spring cover.

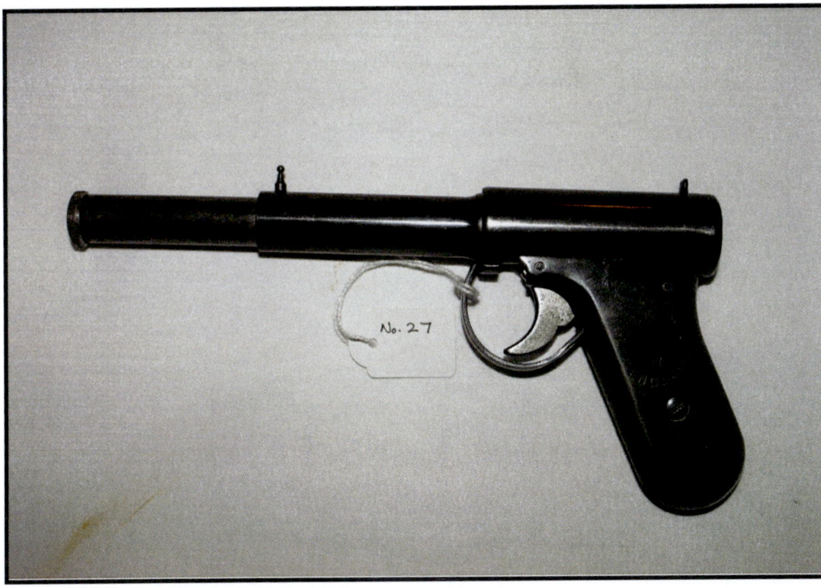

Pistol no.27, left side showing excellent quality blued finish.

Pistol no.27, right grip stamping, very weak towards rear of grip.

Pistol no.27, left grip trademark.

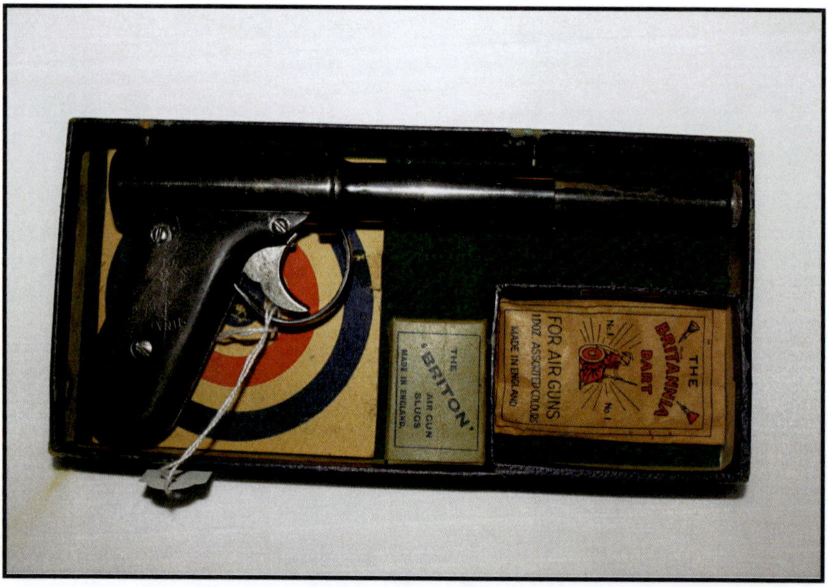

Pistol no.27, in good boxed condition with target, darts and empty pellet box.

Pistol no.27, lid of box, states The Dawn of a New All Steel British Made Air Pistol. Reliable and Strong. With a drawing of a pistol on the box lid that bears little resemblance to the actual pistol inside.

Accessories from pistol no 27, unopened pack of darts and empty pellet box.

Purchasing a selection of manufacturers catalogues from the Internet threw up a very useful advert from the Joseph Bourne and Son 1933 catalogue where the three pistols shown the Garanta, Britannia and Warrior were all described as new lines, 100% British. This would date them as being around 1932 to 1933.

1933 Joseph Bourne and Son catalogue illustration showing the Britannia pistol, note the price of 8s 6d (42 1/2p) for black and 9s (45p) for nickel compared to the 25s (£1.25p) for the Warrior. Of the pistols shown, provided the catalogue is correct in stating that they were new lines, then all were most probably of 1932 manufacture as it would have required some time to produce the catalogue. None appeared to have been made after 1939.

Dimensions.

Overall length. 8 3/4'' 222mm. Weight. 15 1/4oz 436grm.

Values.

A rarish pistol, I paid £130 plus premium at auction for the chrome version and £230 in swappage for the blue example, both boxed, and considered both of those prices to be very reasonable, would have expected to pay more and considerably more for a mint boxed version with all the bits.

Auction. £370 boxed, £120 unboxed.

British Cub pistols.

British Cub pistols are another of the great gat mysteries, the maker or makers are unknown and the date of manufacture is also uncertain. Of the three pistols that were available for examination all have distinct and obvious differences.

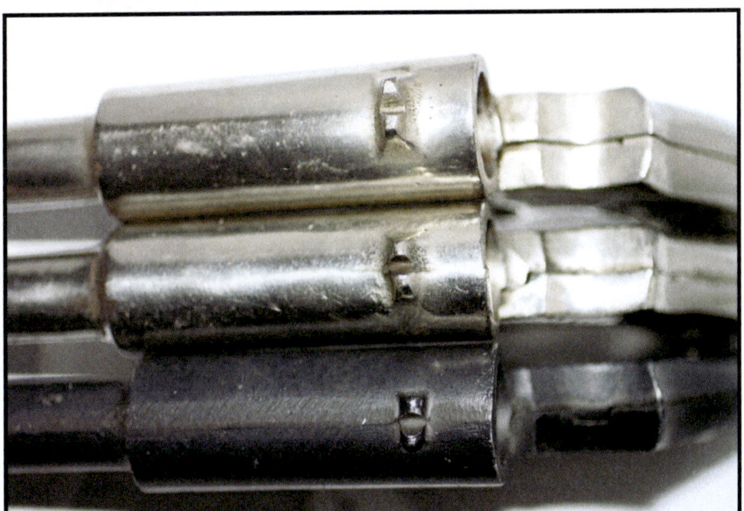

Three pistols viewed from rear and top, oldest (?) on right and on top.

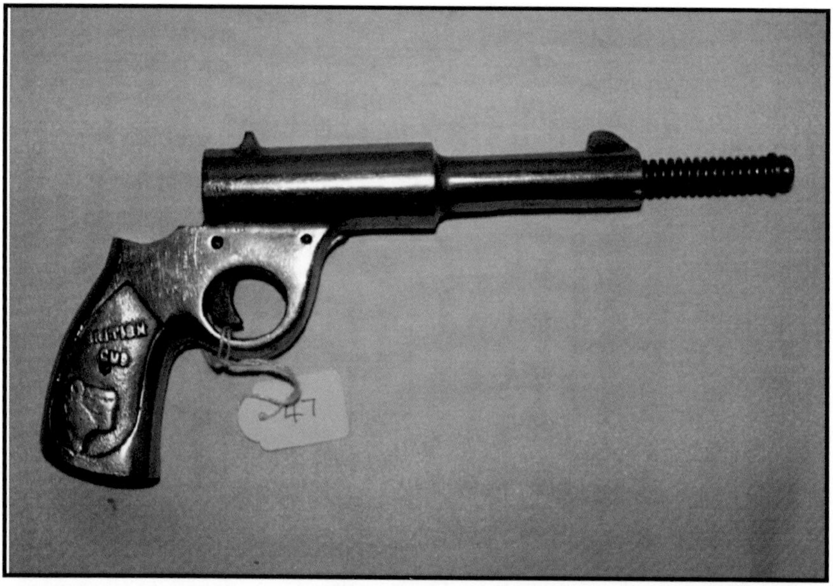

Pistol no. 47, right side, showing the reasonably good degree of nickelled finish.

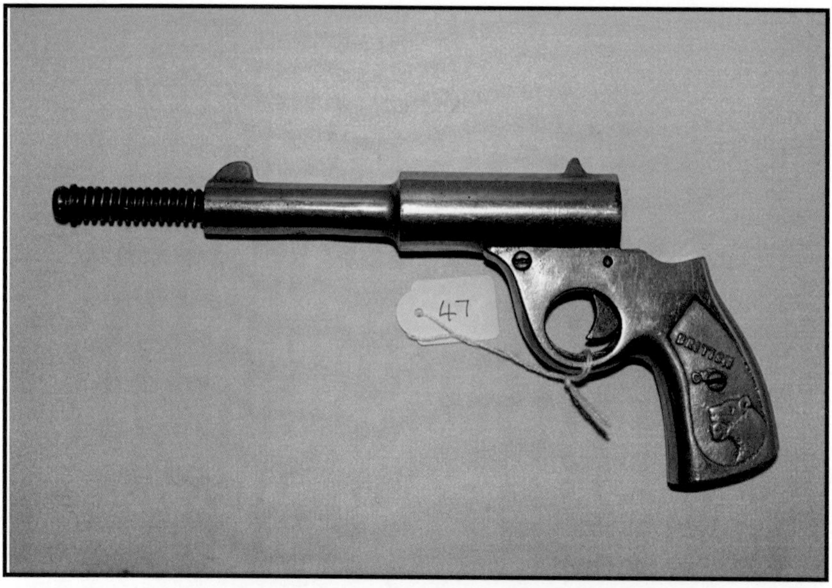

Pistol no. 47, cast iron, note screw through word CUB and diabalo muzzle nut.

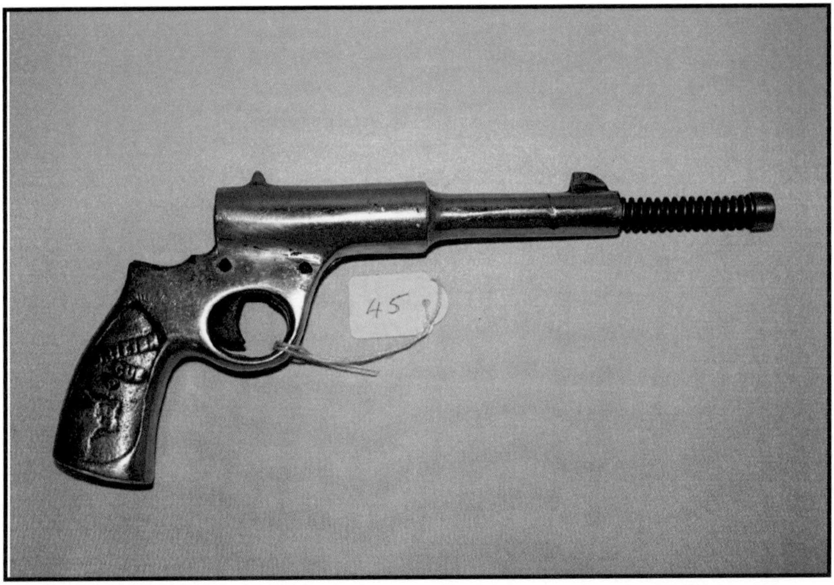

Pistol no. 45, right side, nickelled cast iron, cruder finish than pistol no. 47.

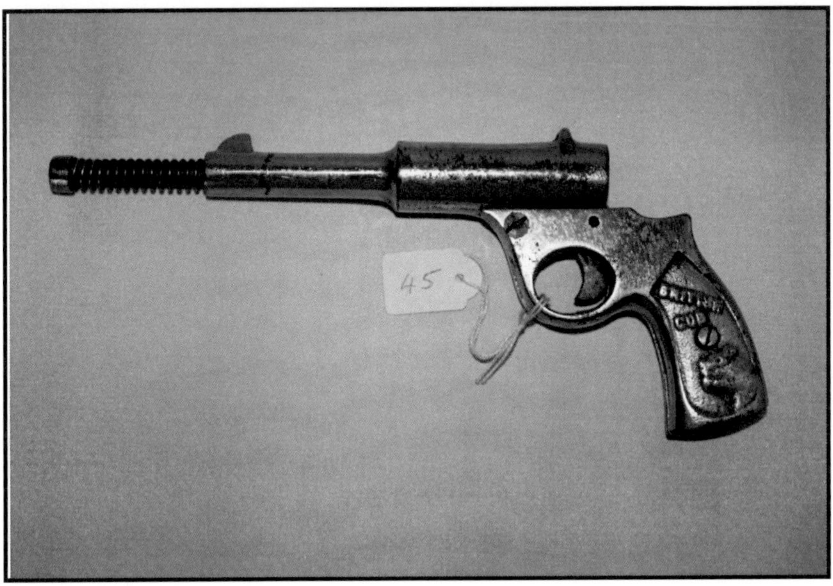

Pistol no. 45, left side, much cruder screws and simple cylindrical muzzle nut.

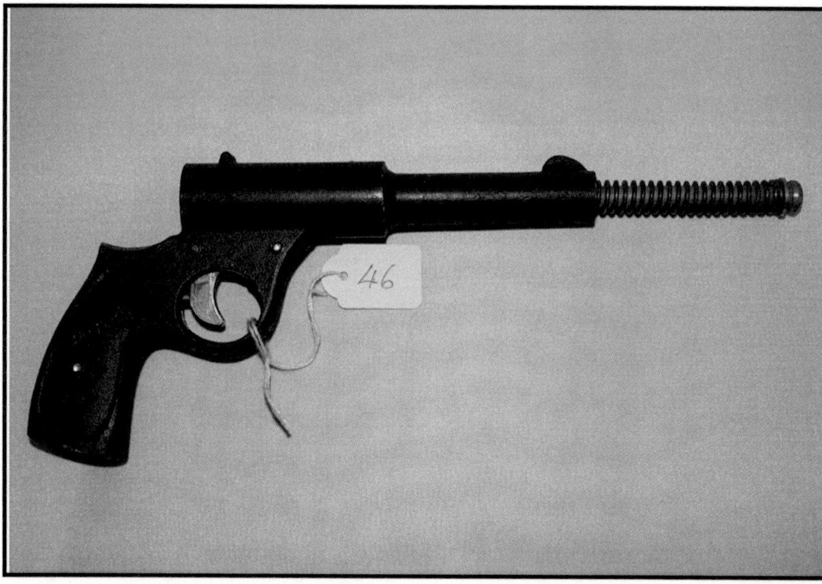

Pistol no. 46, right side, very light alloy pistol, black finished, no lions head.

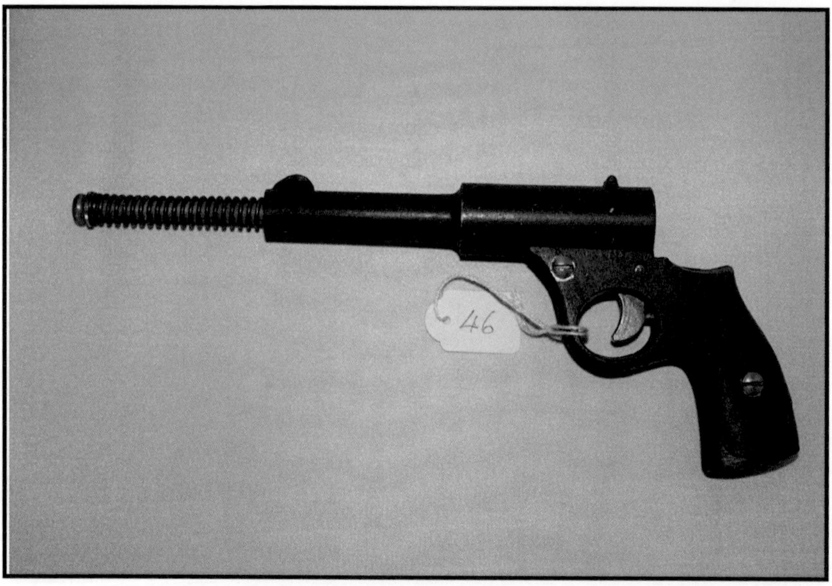

Pistol no. 46, left side, note the crisp casting and the different trigger.

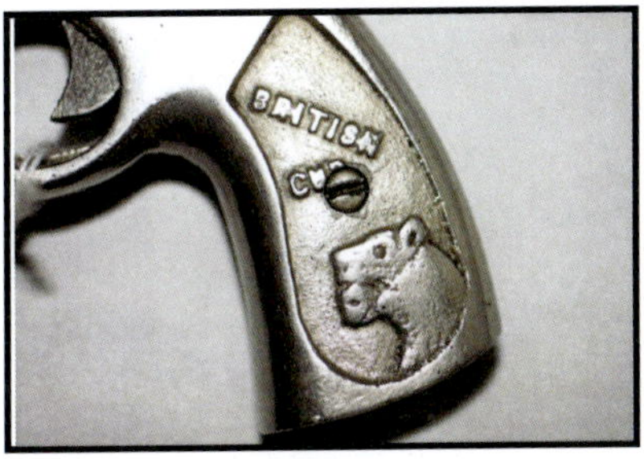

Pistol no. 47, left butt.

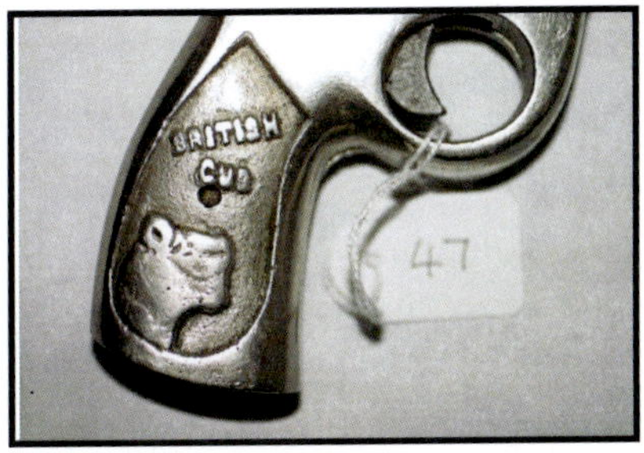

Right butt, note crisp casting detail.

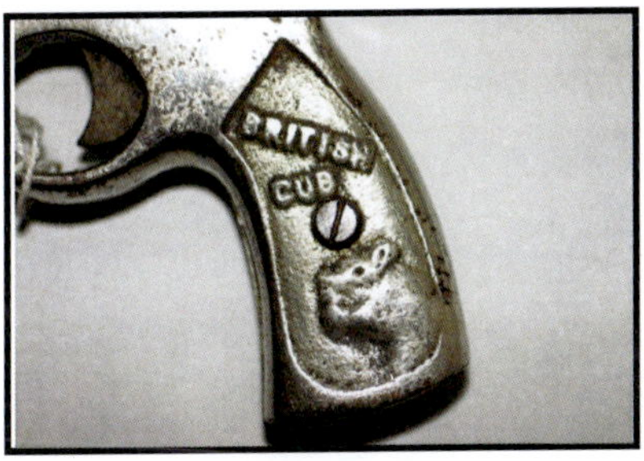

Pistol no. 45, left butt.

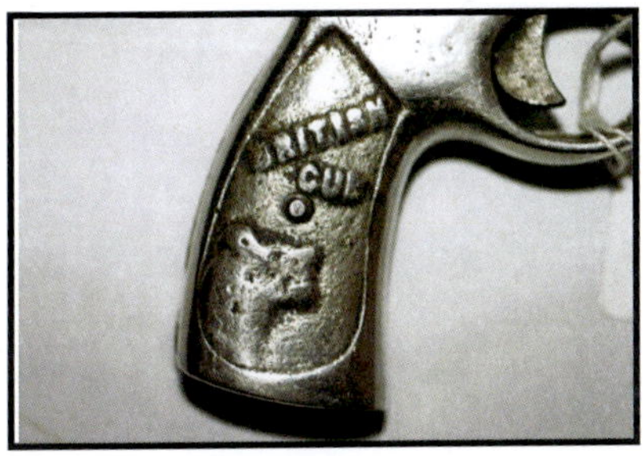

Right butt, note cruder casting details.

Pistol no. 46, left butt.

Right butt, note changes in the design.

History.

At this moment there is very little solid information available about this series of pistols, they may have been produced in Germany or Britain or possibly in both countries. Examination of the pistols gave rise to some tentative ideas, however these may alter as more information comes to light.

Descriptions.

Pistol no. 47, there is a great deal of speculation at the moment regarding this series of pistols. By examination no. 47 would appear to be the oldest and has sufficient similarities to German pistols to almost certainly be ascribed to Germany and of probably pre-war manufacture. Heavier construction and certainly better finished than no. 45, it has different joint lines on top of the butt with crisper lettering and designs.

Pistol no. 45, in comparison with no. 47 this pistol is of much cruder construction, in fact it almost looks like a sand casting taken using a pistol such as no. 47 as a pattern, it may be that is exactly what occurred, in which case if proved, would point towards very early post-war production, possibly in either Germany or Britain.

Pistol no. 46, this pistol is made of blackened, very light aluminium alloy; it is one of the lightest gats encountered and is of a distinctly varied design to the previous pistols. It was almost certainly produced in Britain in the early post war years and made using aluminium due to the chronic post war shortages of brass and steel, civilian use of which was heavily restricted and subject to stringent rationing. This was the period of 'Export or Die' and precious little material was available or even allotted for home consumption. Apart from the extreme lightness this pistol has a different joint above the butt, has a shorter thinner cylinder, a stud protruding from the rear of the trigger to hold the coil return spring and different butt design lacking the lion (or irate pussy cat) head. Estimate date of manufacture as circa 1948.

Conclusion. A very uncommon and elusive pistol. With a possible production period excluding the war period from the mid 1930's to late 1940's. All versions seen have very obvious manufacturing differences. There may well be undiscovered variations still outstanding. They may prove somewhat difficult to find, I was very lucky to persuade a long time collector to part with them.

Dimensions.

Overall length no.47	9 11/16''	246mm.	Weight.	1lb 5 1/4oz	603grm.
Overall length no.45	9 7/8''	251mm.	Weight.	1lb 1 3/4oz	506grm.
Overall length no.46	10 7/16''	266mm.	Weight.	8 1/2oz	240grm.

Values.

Estimated price range of £10 to £80, double if it comes with a good box. Have not seen any others for sale recently.

Auction, £15.

Notes.

British Diana G2's

Although there is evidence of significant pre-war interaction between Diana Germany and various British firms, there is little real evidence to prove which pistols were made where, however it is known is that following WWII in around 1946 to 1947 when armament production in Germany was banned a significant amount of German production machinery was dismantled as war reparation. Mayer & Grammelspacher were in the French sphere of influence but they were not interested and a British investigation team including Millard took over the investigation of the surviving Diana Rastatt plant & machinery.

Whatever the secret negotiations consisted of the details are now lost in the mists of time, but the outcome was very much to the advantage of Millard Brothers & Co. who ended up with the airgun and probably much of the other production machinery that had survived the heavy Allied bombing raids.

Usable machinery and parts were removed to Motherwell in Scotland and set up to continue production of the Diana lines. Fortuitously for Millards they had also acquired the rights to the famous & well regarded Diana trademark, a move that was to cause the German firm severe problems for several decades.

Milbro, which was the alternate trademark of Millard Brothers, was used in conjunction with Diana from about 1948 to 1950 when production started until the firm ceased trading in 1982, shortly afterwards the Diana trademark reverted to the German firm.

Examination of various pistols presented problems as English & German production techniques appear to be almost identical, however looking at British production pistols showed one major difference, which was the recurved shape of the trigger which gave it a squared appearance, most German pistols appear to have a normal crescent curve to the front of the trigger. If this is proved to be correct some of the rib grip tinplate Diana clones may well have been produced pre and post-war by Milbro, see the British Diana G2 section for details.

Given the amount of work required for setting up a new factory and the serious shortages of materials, most of which were restricted to export and rationed severely for the home market in the early post-war years, it is appears unlikely that any serious production took place until the end of the 1940's and probably nothing significant until the very early part of the 1950's.

Production of the Milbro/Diana model G2 pistols appears to have passed through several stages. However initial production may have started off by assembling parts retrieved from Germany, parts being made on older dies with minor parts being made in Scotland, (I admit to this being pure guesswork on my part, however it would seem to be a logical point for starting production).

Pistol no. 83, Early Milbro tinplate possibly pre or just post WW2.

Pistol no. 83, Milbro mark confined to left side rectangle above ribbed grip. Right side rectangle has Made in England stamp. Inserted blade foresight lost and a contemporary repair made using a post type replacement, fitted with re-curved type trigger. Right side Made in England seen on other named pistols.

Pistol no. 83, Stamps in left and right rectangles

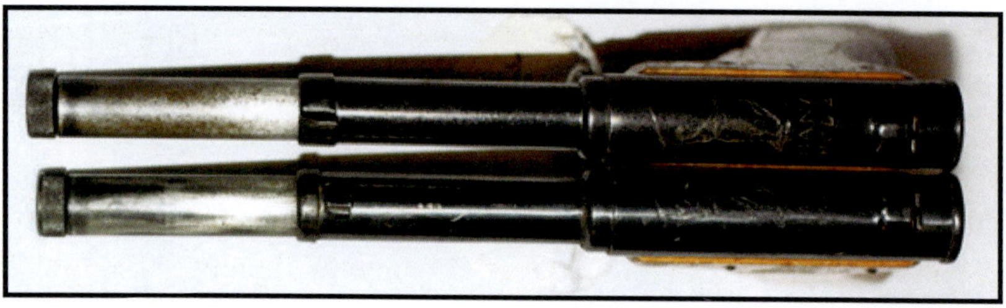

Cylinder cap & foresight of pistol no. 31 compared with pistol no. 20 above it. Note the cap on no. 31 is separate from the inserted foresight, while on pistol no. 20 the sight is press formed from a folded section of the end cap.

Pistol no. 20, early post-war markings.

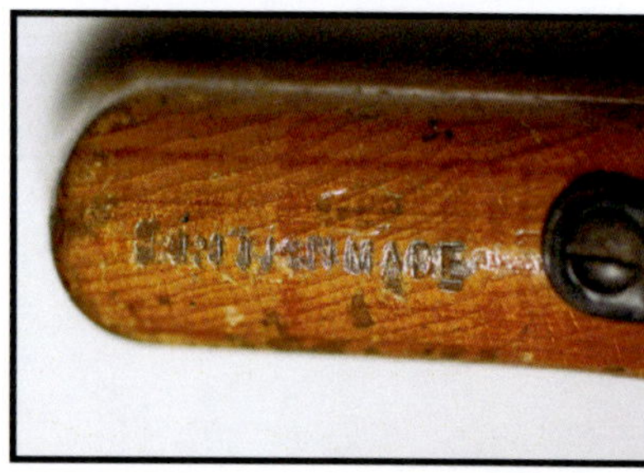

Pistol no. 20, grip front marking.

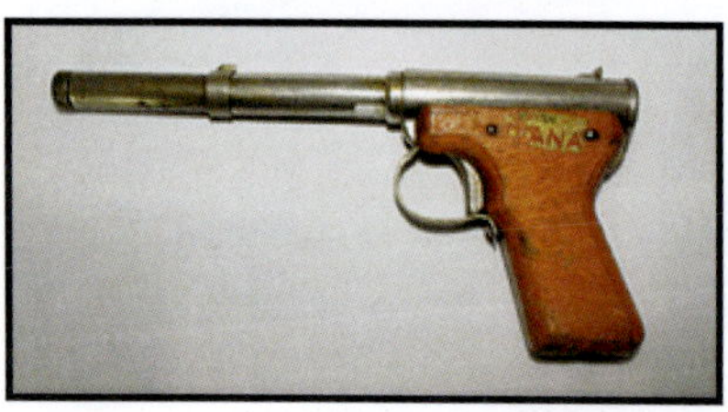

Pistol no. 86, nickel with barrel seam.

Pistol no. 86, transfer on left side.

Pistol no. 20, circa early 1950’s.

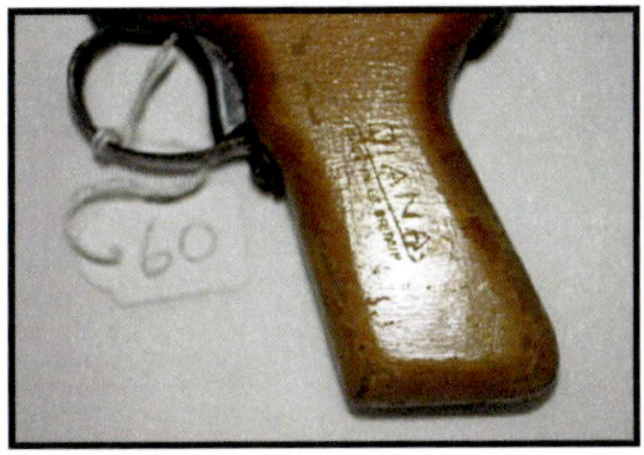

Pistol no. 60, date stamp for 1955.

Pistol no. 21, date stamp for 1956.

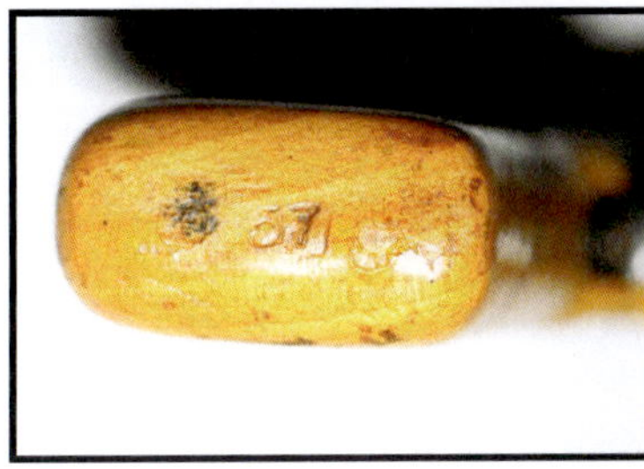

Pistol no. 87, 1957 date stamping.

Pistol no. 87, right side. 1957.

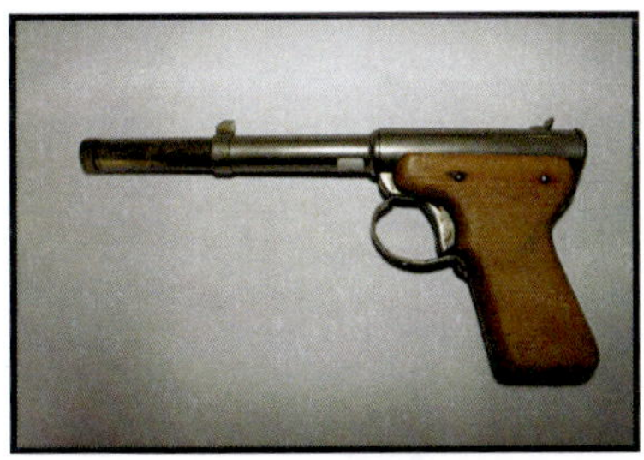

Pistol no. 85, note plain wood grip .

Pistol no. 85, estimated date 1957.

Pistol no. 85, Cylinder markings.

Comparison between the drawn tubing of no. 85 and the seam tubing of no. 86.

Comparison of thick and thin barrel shrouds between pistols no. 84 and 87.

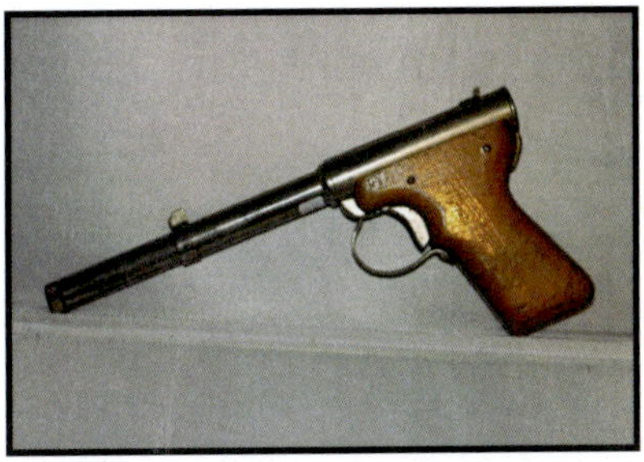

Pistol no. 66, date stamp for 1961.

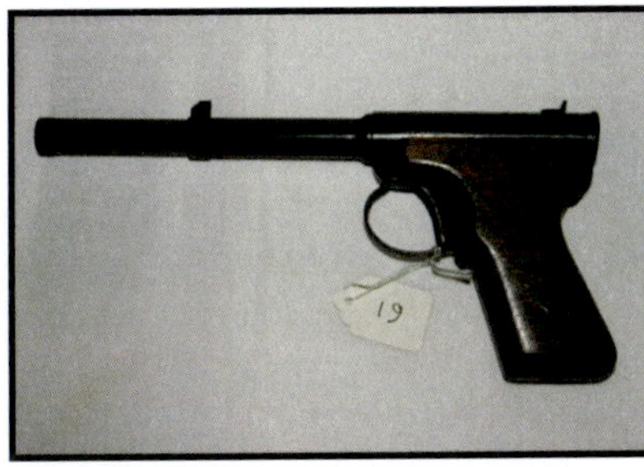

Pistol no.19, larger date stamp 1965.

Pistol no. 22, plastic grip, late 1970's.

Pistol no. 23, late model G2/5 ci. 1981.

Gold paint filled G.B marking.

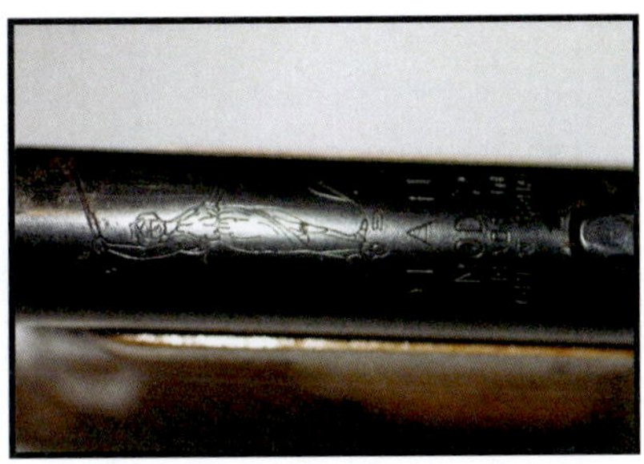

Dull finish, without gold paint infill.

There appeared to be several periods when the gold letter infilling was used and then discontinued, only to be re-instated at a later date. It is noticeable that there were distinct colour and shading differences in the infill and sometimes, even on mint condition pistols the density of colour can vary quite considerably. Also the blueing appears in both bright and dull finishes but not enough examples have been seen of the dull finish to establish a reliable production date.

Description of British G2 pistols, in age order.

Diana, Germany were producing wood gripped versions of the G2 pre-war, British post war production probably started with full tinplate pistols before turning to wooden gripped versions which appear to be stamped on the base of the butt with an possible three number date code, which could to be a batch number followed by what appears to be a two number year code. Placing the various pistols in the best probable order seems to confirm that this is indeed a form of dating system.

Pistol no. 83, out of many tinplate pistols examined this was the earliest found so far that was marked Milbro, left side rectangle above grip stamped Milbro in italics, right side rectangle has Made in England stamp which appears identical to the stamps found on tinplate Britons and Limits. It may be that this is a pre-war pistol, in which case Milbro may well turn out to be the maker of quite a few of the other named pistols. No markings on the top of the cylinder.

Pistol no. 31, Blued with wooden grip secured by blued pins, no marks to suggest production either in Germany or Britain, but it has a re-curved type trigger and very small cylinder shroud end cap with separate inserted foresight behind the cap, which differs from all other versions. Diana huntress trademark on cylinder with small mod 2 beneath, possibly this is a late production German pistol transferred to Milbro or one assembled from parts from both countries. It has to be remembered that Britain was nearly bankrupt in terms of funds and materials following the War and anything that could be sold or especially exported was seized upon with alacrity.

Pistol no. 20, Blued with light colour wooden grip secured by blued pins, unfortunately the butt stamp is unclear but estimate it to be early 1950's, front of butt stamped British Made, re-curved type trigger, gold filled huntress with larger Mod 2 on cylinder. Foresight pressed out of the barrel cap, this pistol may represent the first type of wooden grip pistol produced totally in Scotland.

Pistol no. 86, circa 1953 nickel or chrome with seamed barrel, very low foresight pressed out of barrel cap, wooden grip with plated pins, impact damage has obscured the dating code, but the cylinder markings include the Huntress trademark over DIANA and MOD 2 but exclude the Made in Great Britain lines, instead there are the remains of a gold-size type transfer on the left side of the butt between the pins with British Diana in black and red lettering.

Pistol no. 60, Blue with duller finish, light colour wooden grip secured by blue steel pins, date stamp for 1955, quite similar to no. 20 except trademark not gold filled, Diana with much wider spacing between letters, Mod 2 as no. 20 but with the addition of Made in Great Britain in two lines beneath. Additional Diana stamping on left side of grip.

Pistol no. 21, Blued with slightly darker wooden grip with prominent grain secured by blue steel pins, date stamp for 1956, details much as no. 60 except it has returned to the much brighter blued finish and lost the grip stamping.

Pistol no. 87, blued with wooden grip date stamped for 1957, cylinder top markings comprise Huntress trademark over DIANA above MOD 2 above Made in Great Britain in two lines.

Pistol no. 85, finish appears to be nickel rather than chrome with pale wooden grips, unfortunately the butt stamps are unreadable due to damage but the barrel shroud is a seamless tube and the construction matches pistol no. 87 which is dated as 1957. Cylinder top markings comprise MILBRO above MOD 2 above Made in Great Britain in two lines.

Pistol no. 66, Nickel or chrome plated with lighter colour wood grips secured by blued steel pins, date stamped for 1961, re-curved trigger, seems to have seamless tubing for the under part of the chamber/barrel shroud, most others seem to have an open seam underneath, markings as no. 21. Plated Milbro/Diana G2's appear to be much more uncommon than say chrome Gat's, although it has to be said that the Korean War had caused a worldwide shortage of Nickel and Chromium that lasted well into the late 1950's and any that was available would have been earmarked for heavy industry, even the British motorcycle industry, a major producer during the period was forced to use painted wheel rims and fuel tanks at the time with a minimum of plated trim.

Pistol no. 77, not illustrated, chrome plated with slightly darker wood grips, this pistol has seamless tubing, most blued ones seen have a joint seam under the barrel casing, probably later than no. 66, hard to tell as the date stamping has been obscured due to the pistol being used as a hammer by some nitwit but there are slight differences. Estimate date of manufacture at around 1963.

Pistol no. 19, Blued with dark stained wooden grip secured by blued steel pins, date stamped for 1965 with larger sized numbers, gold filled huntress trademark with markings as no. 21.

Pistol no. 22, modernised shaped black plastic chequered grip secured by three cross bolts with nuts inset in right side of grip, metal work and markings as later wood grip versions, wide dark coloured alloy cast trigger, this may be either the model G2/3 or G2/4, if we presume the tinplate grip version to be G2/1 and the wooden gripped G2/2. Estimated production mid 1970's till 1980, this is pistol seems to make up the majority of the plastic grip versions that are available.

Pistol no. 23, this version was illustrated in the 1981 JLS catalogue and was described as the G2/5. Given that the catalogue required some time to be produced this pistol could date from 1980 indicating a short lifespan as Milbro ceased trading in 1982. Blued with black plastic grip, butt and rear cylinder as no.21 but has a straight tube for the front of the cylinder in a duller blue finish with a PVC or Nylon support for the spring tube, PVC foresight appears to be inserted from beneath and may be formed as part of the bearing for the barrel.

Diana G2 accessories.

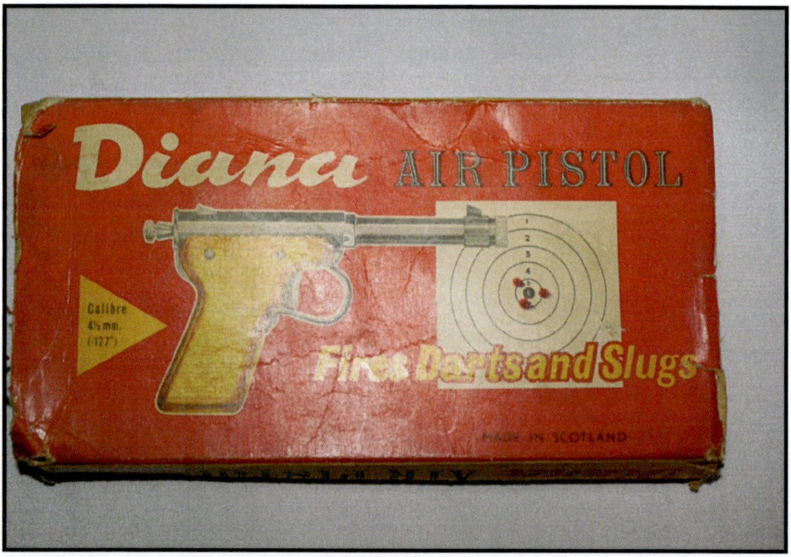

Mid 1960's to 70's box for Diana (Milbro) G2 pistol.

What can I say about the box for the pistol, it should have had a label inside saying which pistol it belonged to, but someone put the box into storage and lost the label (OK it was me!) so sorry but the date is just an estimate.

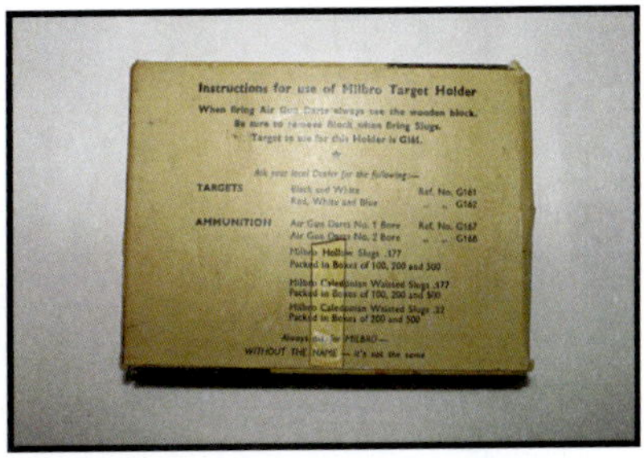

Diana/Milbro target holder, box code dated G262, taken to be 1962 for G2.

1962 Diana/Milbro target holder. Original target, box front and rear of holder.

A box, depending on condition will add about 20 to 50% to the value of a G2, but it won't be a major lottery win.

Target holder on the other hand appears to be an aftermarket purchase as for the life of me I cannot recall small sized target holders in boxes being included in any of the presentation packages of most junior type air rifles, although substantially made it would not hang on the wall for long if hit by an BSA Airsporter or Webley Mark 3!, as far as I know none of the Diana pistols were ever sold with a target holder included. Holder is pretty common but packaging is certainly heading towards chicken teeth territory.

Addresses.

Milbro/Millard Brothers operated from their London addresses both pre and post war, why the post war factory was established in Scotland appears something of a mystery, but one suggestion is that it was to provide jobs in what was a becoming a very depressed area, following the rapid decrease in demand after urgent and essential war production work ceased when the war ended.

Addresses.

There were differing addresses throughout the period of Milbro operations. There may be more addresses and some of those below may have been in use at the same time.

1960 to mid 1963. Millard Bros. Diana Works, Carfin, Motherwell. Scotland.

October 1962. Diana Works, Carfin, Motherwell. and 467 Caledonian Road. London. N7.

Mid 1963 on. Millard Bros. Ltd. Lanarkshire, Scotland. (also seen without Ltd).

Early 70's. Milbro Sports Ltd. U.K. and Milbro Millard Brothers Ltd. P.O. Box 24. Motherwell, Lanarkshire. ML1 4UP.

1978 on. Milbro Dept. C. Millard Bros. Ltd. P.O.Box 24, Motherwell, Lanarkshire. ML1 4UP. Southern Sales Office, 30 Wates Way, Micham, Surrey. CR4 4HR.

Dimensions.

Tinplate version.

Overall length.	9 13/16''	250mm.	Weight.	11 3/8oz	325grm.

Wood grip version.

Overall length.	9 13/16''	250mm.	Weight.	10 1/8oz	302grm.

Values.

Pistol values, range from free to around £50 for mint boxed version with a premium for a plated pistol, however most of these pistols were used and abused and seem to be a target for amateur carpenters and bodgers, who's lack of anything remotely resembling skill is sometimes astonishing.

Normal values lie in the £10 to £25 range.

Auction. £10, £10, £5, £15, £15, £5, £15 & £12.

Value of target holder between 50p and £5 depending on condition, could be asked up to £30 for a mint boxed example, in lightly used condition in slightly worn box as shown around £10 to £20 would be a fair retail price.

Auction. None have appeared.

Notes.

Wood butt pistol butt securing pins have also been seen in brass, but not in sufficient quantity to establish a dating period so far.

Briton pistols including Super Briton.

The earliest Briton pistol seems to have been either of cast iron or heavy steel and was made in the early1920's to 1930's. In appearance it was very similar to the Scout air pistol and was made without a trigger guard, it may well be a cheaper version made by the same as yet not positively identified manufacturer.

Of slightly later manufacture than the above, but possibly made in parallel prior to WWII was a heavy steel and tinplate version with trigger guard which was quickly superseded by a tinplate ribbed grip Diana Model 2 clone. Some of these pistols may well have been made by Dianawerke Germany under contract. Pistol no.17 has many of the attributes of a German made pistol but given the re-curved type of trigger was probably made in very early post war Britain.

Pistol no. 34, has off white inserted plastic grip panels, this can probably be given a date about 1948 – 50 and is almost certainly British. There was a serious post war shortage of steel. Hence the inserted plastic grips. An almost identical but slightly lighter Limit pistol has the same type of inserted grip but in a mottled brown colour, the Limit may have come from the same maker.

Pistol no. 80, originally blued with plated trigger, made without trigger-guard.

Pistol no. 80, right side view, fitted with large headed nickelled pusher pin.

Pistol no. 80, Right grip details.

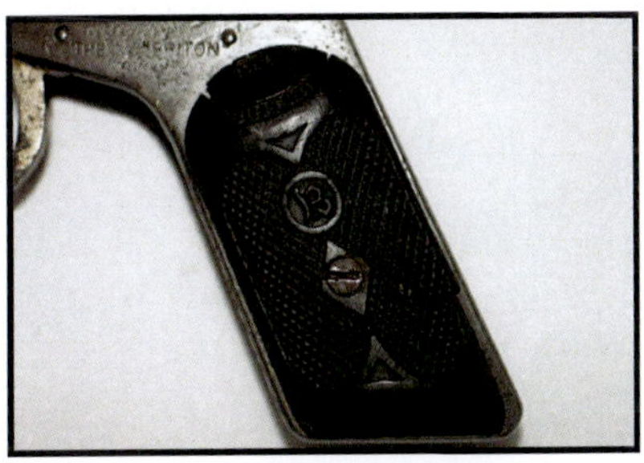

Pistol no. 80, Left grip details.

Pistol no.17, blued tinplate, almost identical to Diana Model 2.

Pistol no. 17, left side of pistol, note re-curved shape of trigger.

Pistol no. 34, with white grips, note copper packing washers under screw heads.

Pistol no. 80 represents the earliest form of Briton so far discovered, it was made without a trigger guard from around 1920 to 1925 when a version with what looks like a spring steel guard was produced until about 1930, the only difference was a small hole through the frame forward of the trigger to secure the guard with a cross pin. No. 80 had a blued finish with the trigger and pellet pusher in bright nickel plate. Grips, like the Scout pistol appear to be of pressed laminated horn and have cracked and delaminated with age, luckily without serious losses. The grips vary on either side, both having a gothic 'B' in a circle trademark above the securing screw, the top of the right grip has Made in England while the top of the left grip is marked The Briton.

All the Briton pistols since the introduction of the tinplate versions have a cylinder stamping of a particularly strange bulldog that looks as if it's been licking wee off a stinging nettle. Earlier pistols have line shading on the dog's belly which seems to disappear on the later versions of the pistol.

As well as the Briton there was also a Super Briton version, described as 'all steel British pistol', however the construction of this pistol is very similar to the post war Dolla Mk 2, distinct similarities are found in the overall dimensions, barrel shape and especially the two holes in the rear of the piston either side of the pellet push pin, this was used with a pin spanner to strip the Dolla Mk 2 from the rear, however the pistol below also has a removable muzzle nut to use when stripping down the barrel unit. Possibly, contract made by Anchutz.

Pistol no. 50, Super Briton marking on left side only, dog stamp on front band.

Pistol no. 50, top band stamping, this stamp appears on the Model 2 type tinplate Briton pistols just in front of the rear sight.

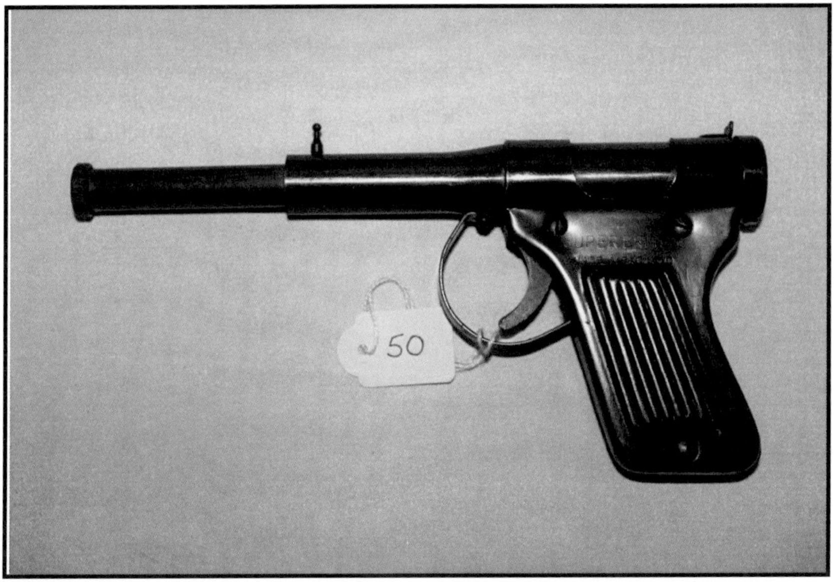

Pistol no. 50, Left side view, note solid steel trigger and post foresight.

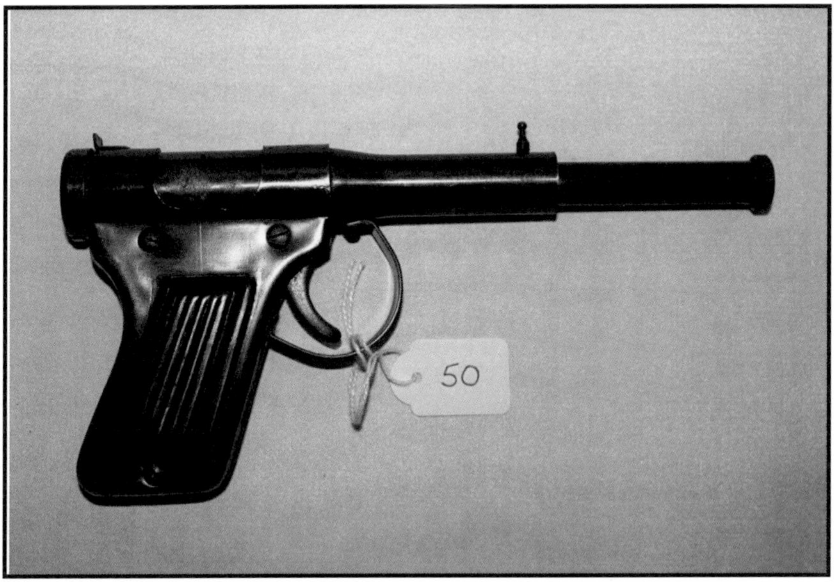

Pistol no. 50, right side view.

It is obvious that the top forward cylinder band of the Super Briton (no. 50) has been stamped with a standard Briton stamp, however the left hand side stamping above the grip seems to be much less crisp, in fact it looks positively weak. Is it possible that this was intended to be an improved version of the Briton but was too expensive and gained the Super Briton title in order to sell at a higher price?

None of the pistols examined showed any indication of the actual manufacturer, this also includes whatever boxes that have been seen, it is more than probable that a lot of these pistols were sold by retailers and different model names were applied at the request of or by the sellers and only appeared on the package labelling, even at this date there also seemed to be a lot of interchange between the various manufacturers, who may well have been producing batches of pistols and air rifles for their so called rivals.

Dimensions.

Cast Iron / Steel Briton.

Overall length. 8 3/8'' 218mm. W 11 3/8 oz 322 grm.

Tinplate Briton with inserted plastic grips.

Overall length. 9 7/8'' 251mm. Weight. 11 1/2 oz 328 grm.

Super Briton.

Overall length. 8 1/8'' 207mm. Weight. 12 1/2 oz 353 grm.

Values.

Cast Iron Briton, rare, probably £50 to £200, seen early 2011 at £250

Auction. None have appeared.

Intermediate heavy steel Briton, seen early 2011 at £125.

Auction. None have appeared.

Briton, pre-war and post war prices are not too different, all should be within the £10 to £100 range depending on condition, more if boxed.

Auction. £80

Super Briton, much rarer than the Briton, and very much harder to find in good condition, near mint example above cost a significant amount of swappage, at around the £250 mark, so estimate price range as £50 to £300 or more for a boxed example.

Auction. None have appeared.

Notes.

Additional details were found on Pistol no. 74, tinplate construction, very similar to no. 17, but has lost inserted foresight and misaligned dog stamping lacks belly hairs. The pistol has a black enamel paint finish which appears to be contemporary with a re-curving trigger pointing to very late British manufacture.

Cast Iron Dolla's.

Mostly produced in Germany, with production starting around the 1890's, there are many variations in butt and trigger designs but very few differences in the cylinder and barrel. Unfortunately not many of these pistols carry any sort of identification and the same pistols were advertised under different names by different retailers, the apparent lack of markings could be because they were supplied to the trade at such a low price and in such a competitive market that the addition of the few extra pennies to add markings might reduce sales.

Early pistols can be identified by a straight back to the trigger guard opening which was supposedly in production until around 1933, the oval type opening which superseded it lasting until WW2, however going by the amount of oval opening pistols in existence, I have a feeling that the oval type may have been in production prior to 1933. The robust build quality of these cheap pistols has ensured a high survival rate with the oval type appearing to be the most common, something that appears to be at odds with the supposed limited production period.

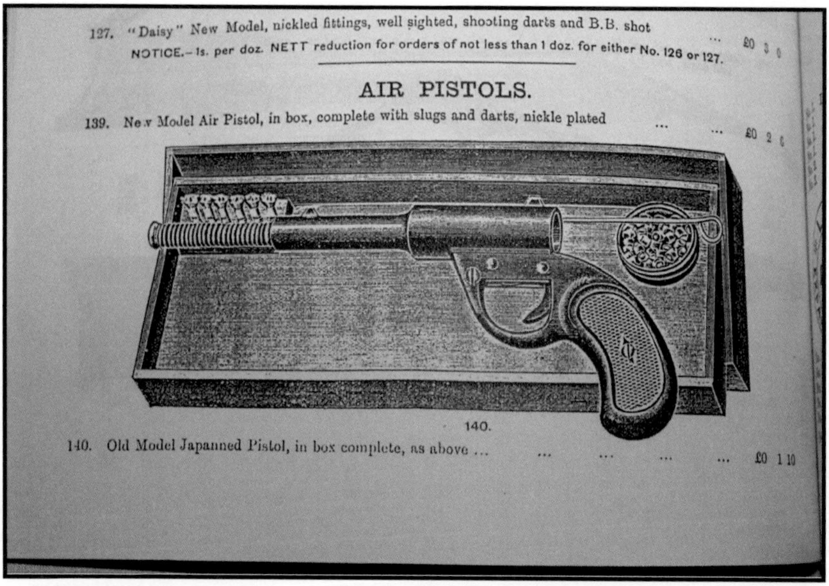

Advert from undated Frank Dyke and Co. trade advert circa 1900.

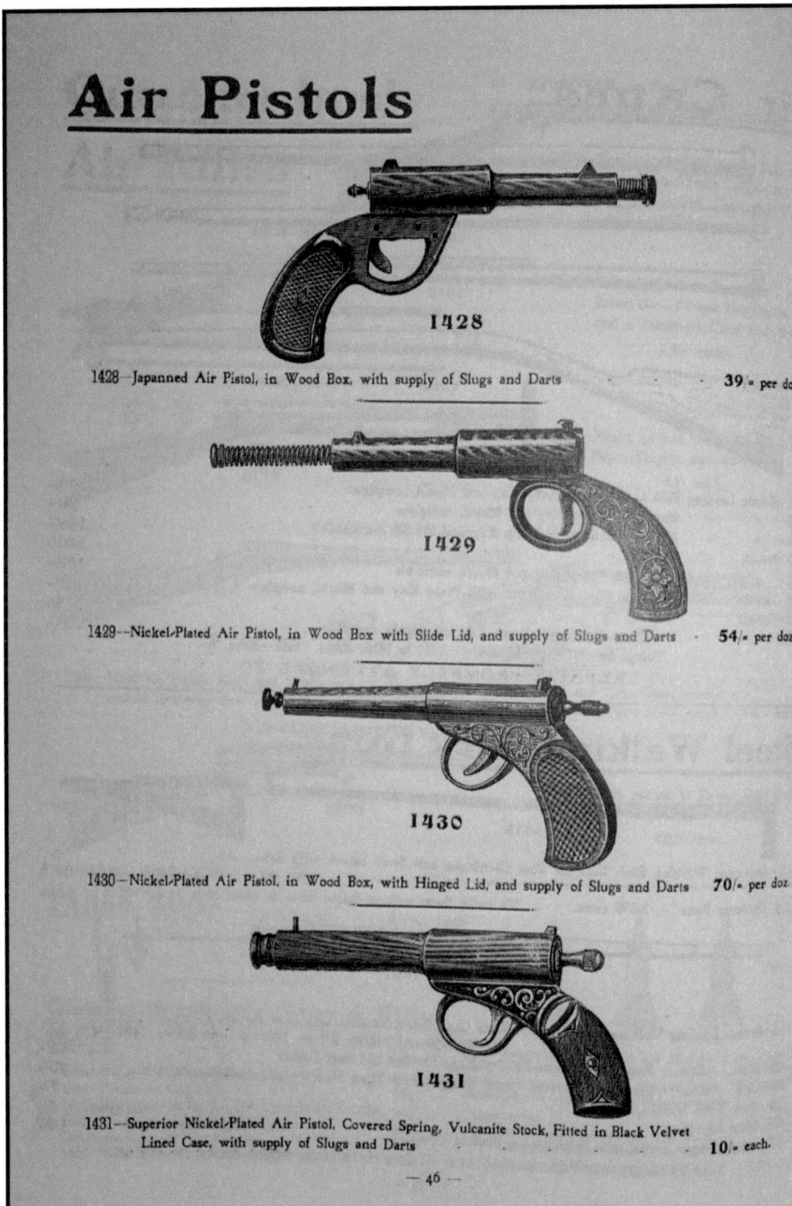

Air Pistols

1428

1428—Japanned Air Pistol, in Wood Box, with supply of Slugs and Darts - - - - 39/- per do

1429

1429—Nickel-Plated Air Pistol, in Wood Box with Slide Lid, and supply of Slugs and Darts - 54/- per doz

1430

1430—Nickel-Plated Air Pistol, in Wood Box, with Hinged Lid, and supply of Slugs and Darts 70/- per doz.

1431

1431—Superior Nickel-Plated Air Pistol, Covered Spring, Vulcanite Stock, Fitted in Black Velvet Lined Case, with supply of Slugs and Darts - - - - - - - 10/- each.

— 46 —

Advert from Charles Osbourne & Co. 1905 catalogue showing gat type pistols.

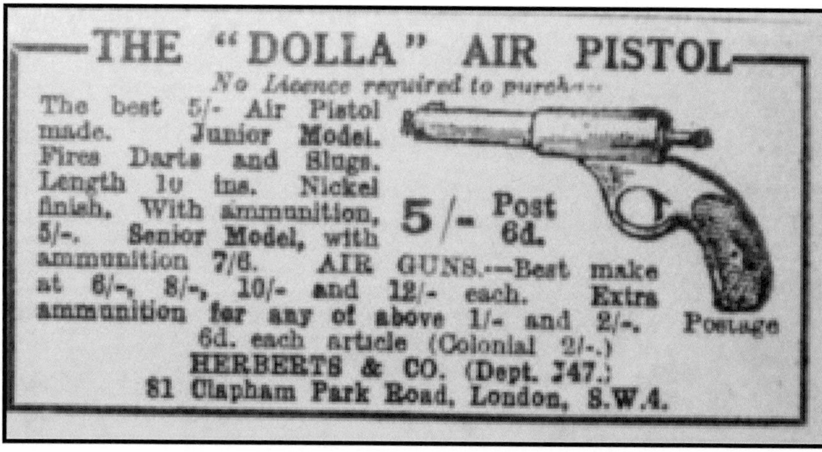

Advert from 1937 copy of Boys Own magazine for two different Dolla's, the normal Dolla described as the Junior Model at 5/- (25p) nickelled and the un-illustrated Senior at 7/6d (37 1/2p), presumably the Senior is a larger, heavier version. I wish today's postal charges were still at these prices!.

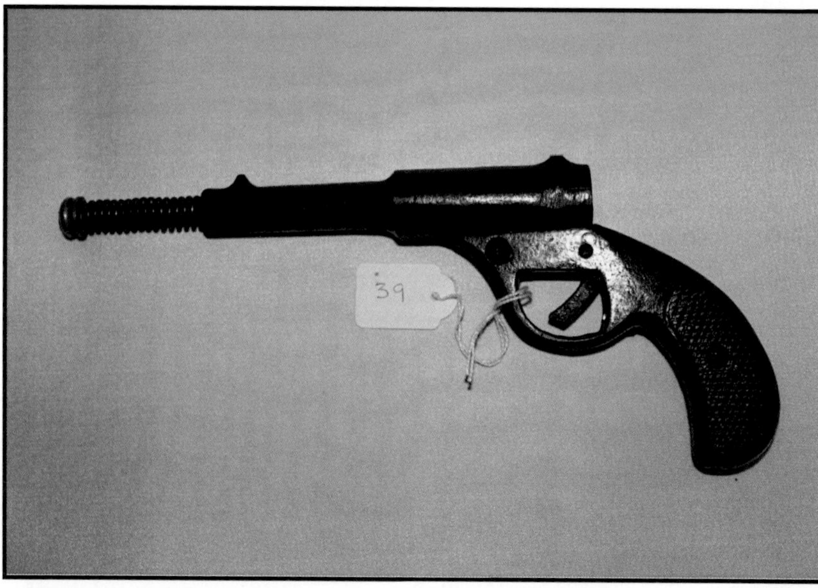

Pistol no.39, left side of very early Dolla possibly pre 1900, no markings.

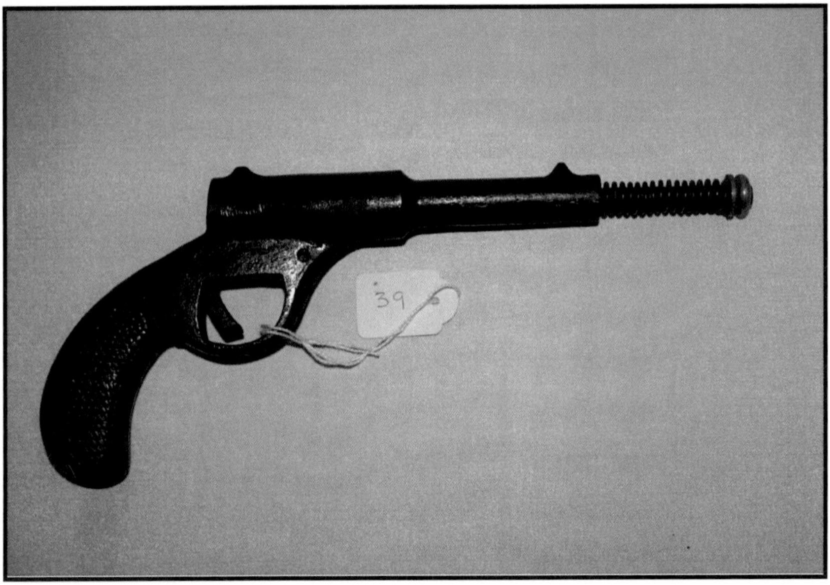

Pistol no. 39, note pyramid foresight and slim trigger.

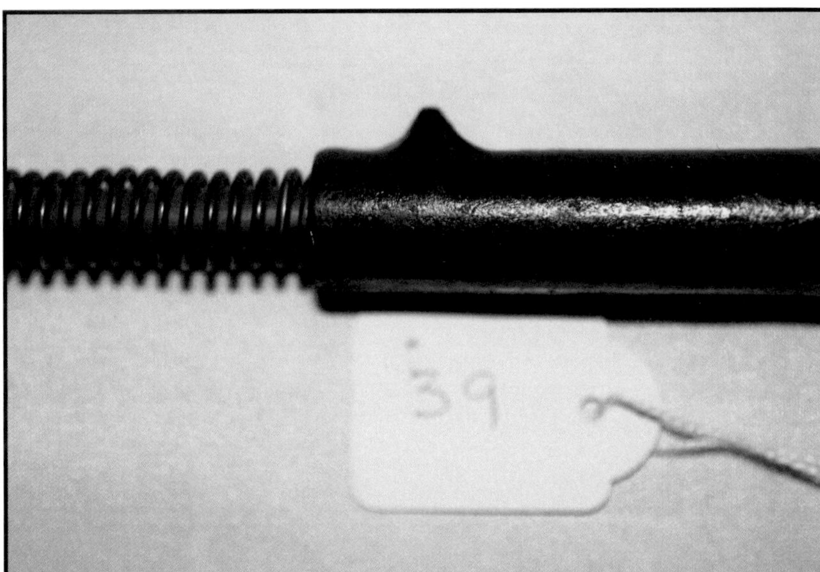

Pistol no. 39, detail of pyramid foresight.

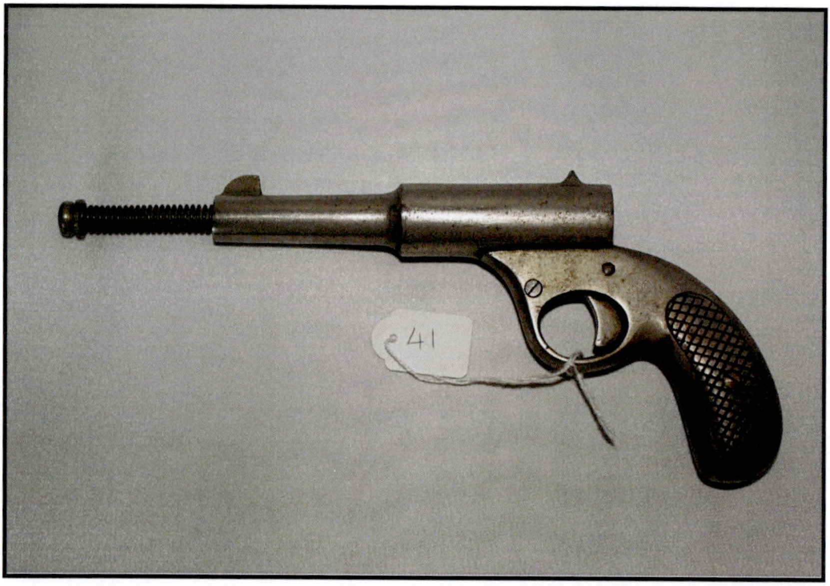

Pistol no. 41, nickel plated, post1933? 2 securing screws, cast marks inside butt.

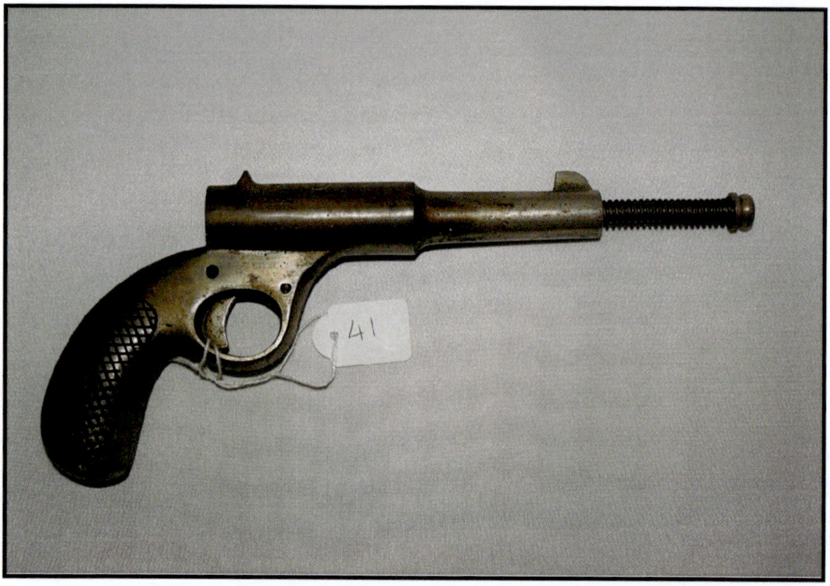

Pistol no. 41, nickel plated with rounded butt.

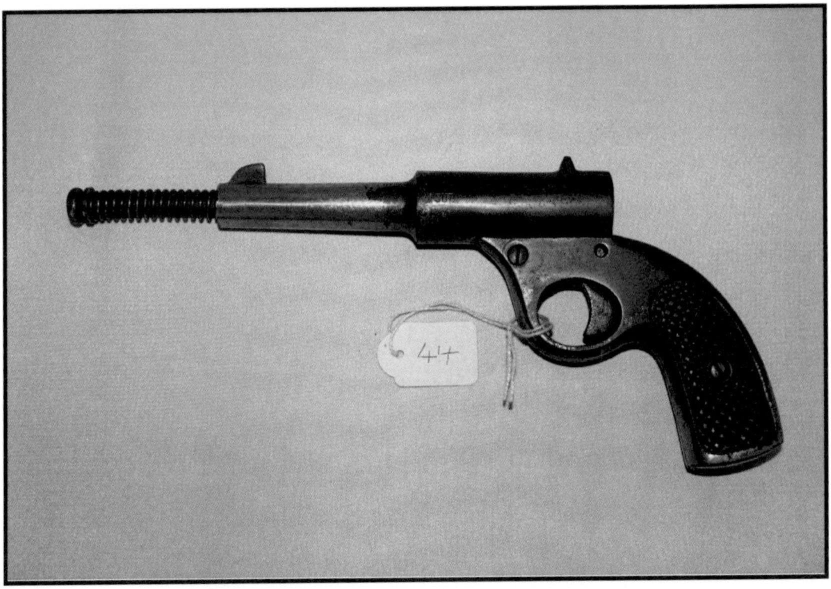

Pistol no. 44, marked CUB, nickelled, 2 screws securing side plate.

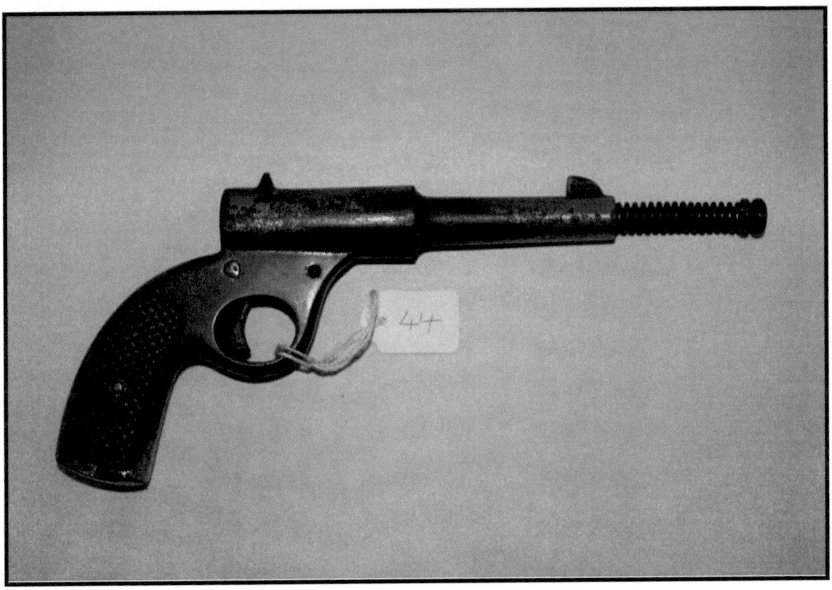

Pistol no. 44, marked CUB, nickelled with flat butt.

Pistol no. 44, CUB stamping on left front of cylinder.

Pistol no. 43, left side, note shorter air chamber and flattened butt.

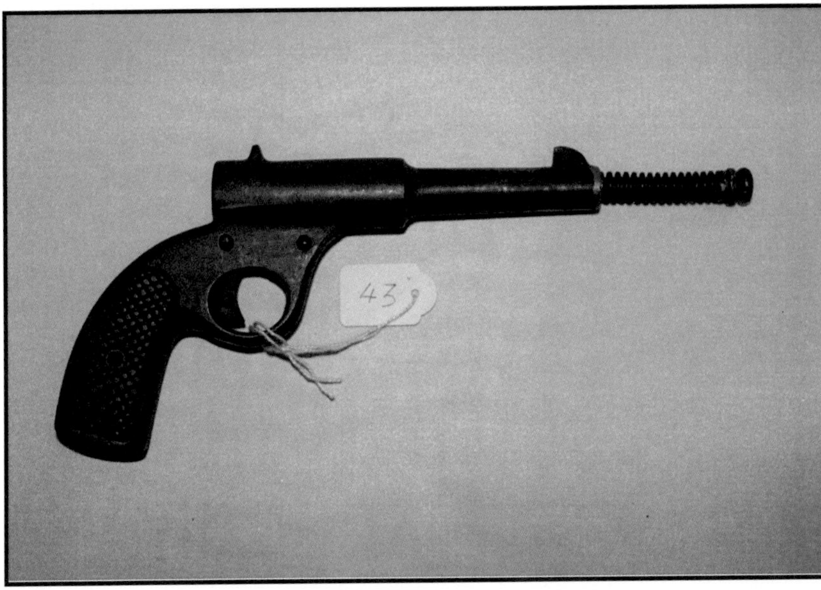

Pistol no. 43, originally nickelled, note shorter air chamber.

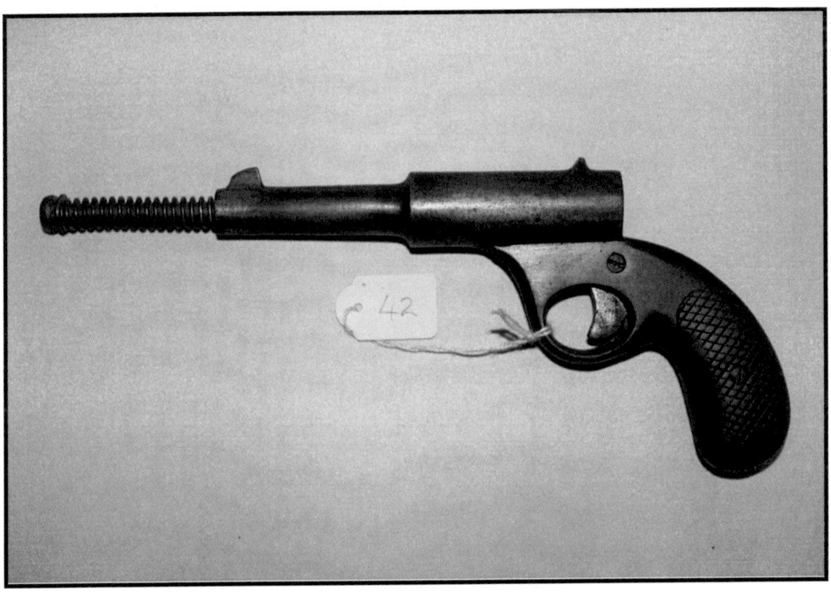

Pistol no. 42, left side, note no screw fitted above front of trigger guard.

Pistol no.42, right side, note securing screw passes through trigger.

Pistol no. 40, distressed black japanned finish.

Descriptions.

These pistols are all of basically similar construction, however there does appear that there are two different lengths of air cylinder, measuring from the rear of the cylinder to the start of the curved portion leading down to the barrel section of the castings, the pistols seem to fall into two groups one of 65 to 68mm and the other 71 to 72mm, it may be that this is the difference between the Junior and Senior versions. Another difference is found on the rear of the butts, pistols 39, 43 & 44 have a square section location peg helping to locate the two butt halves whereas pistols 14, 40, 41 & 42 have straight edges to the butt halves.

Pistol no. 39, early type with squared back to trigger hole. Virtually identical to the pistol in the Frank Dyke and Company advert, circa 1900. This early pistol is of lighter construction than the later ones and has a smaller 65mm diameter cylinder, also of note is the description in the advert of this as the Old pattern with the unfortunately not illustrated no. 139 above it being described as the New pattern, is this perhaps the start of what later becomes the Junior and Senior patterns which are mentioned in the Boys Own advert for 1937.

Pistol no. 41, nickel plated, post 1933? oval trigger hole with blade foresight, no visible external markings, round butt frame, trigger has separate pivot pin instead of integral cast pivots, has three roughly shield shaped indented marks, one above the other inside each grip, flat edges to rear butt joint.

Pistol no. 14, not shown, polished finish, originally black, oval trigger hole also has similar casting marks inside butt to no. 41 which would suggest both were made by the same firm, flat edges to rear butt joint.

Pistol no. 44, Cub pistol attributed to F.R.Langenham, Germany. Nickelled with flat bottomed butt, oval trigger hole, cast trigger pivots, sear fitted with a G shaped return spring, not seen on other pistols, no internal markings. Short 67mm cylinder marked CUB on front left side, other pistols known to have Made in Germany in small letters on the right side, pegged joint at rear of butt.

Pistol no. 43, nickelled with flat base butt, oval guard, squared chequering to butt, no external or internal markings, 68mm air chamber shorter than normal with square pegged joint on back of butt.

Pistol no. 42, originally nickelled with round butt, similar to most other oval guard pistols except for lack of forward securing screw which instead passes through the trigger and acts as a pivot. Chequering polished away at grip front. Internal markings, C cast into base of left grip, D into base of right grip, flat edges to rear butt joint, assume this to be a late production pistol circa 1937.

Pistol no. 40, worn black japanned paint finish, round butt with flat edges to rear butt joint, long 72mm cylinder.

It is noticeable that earlier pistols appear to have a pyramid foresight while later ones have a larger blade.

The name Dolla, which is supposedly based on the price being five shillings when there were four U.S.A. dollars to the pound, probably did not start being used until after WW1 as the advertised prices were significantly less than five shillings up to that time. There is little information as yet as to the differences between the Junior and Senior, but at the moment the slightly longer air chamber and heavier weight could be the only way to identify the Senior model.

Dimensions.

Overall no.43.	9 7/8"	250mm.	Weight.	1lb 1 3/4 oz	499 grm.
Overall no.44.	9 7/8"	250mm.	Weight.	1lb 1 3/4 oz	499 grm.
Overall no.39.	9 1/2"	242mm.	Weight.	14 oz	397 grm.
Overall no.40.	10"	254mm.	Weight.	1lb 3 1/8 oz	541 grm.
Overall no.42.	10"	254mm.	Weight.	1lb 2 oz	510 grm.
Overall no.14.	10 1/16"	257mm.	Weight.	1lb 2 1/4 oz	516 grm.
Overall no.41.	9 15/16"	252mm.	Weight.	1lb 2 1/2 oz	524 grm.

Values.

These pistols can attract highly variable prices, condition makes a huge difference to the price, varying from £15 to over £250 for a mint boxed version.

Auction. £180, £120, £25, £20, £30 & £60. Prices above £100 usually mean a boxed example or an unboxed pistol in exceptional condition.

Notes.

The pistol shown as 1430 in the 1905 Charles Osbourne catalogue advert appears in the 1895 Chums magazine, it also appears in the 1910 Clyde catalogue renamed as the Clyde air pistol.

A late addition, a Dolla turned up complete with a holster, possibly home made, but equally it could be a cheap commercial item.

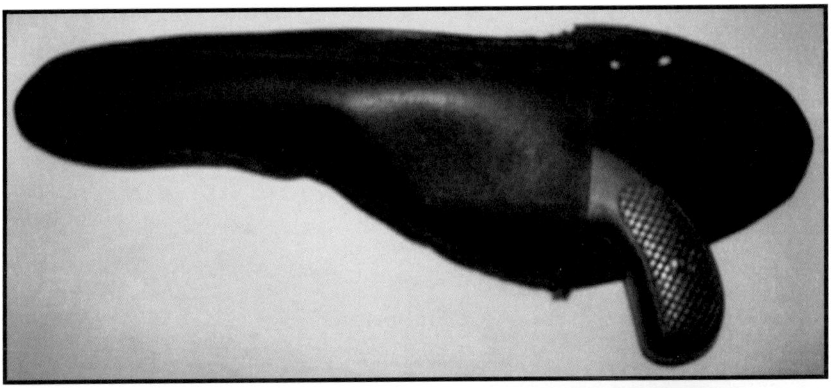

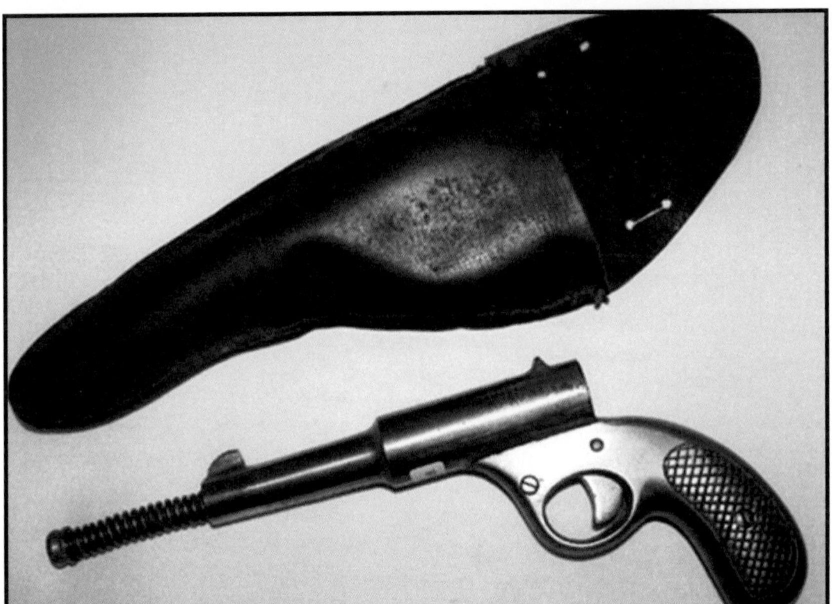

Diana SP50 pistols.

Made as the Diana by Milbro, also under different names by other makers.

The G3/1, quickly renamed the SP50 pistol, was an attempt by Milbro/Diana (which coincided with similar efforts by other firms) to update their older range of gats to a more modern appearance and possibly more economic production. The SP50 was produced as the Diana from the early 1970's until 1982 when Millard Brothers ceased trading and was possibly made during that period with other names attached. It seems that it did not completely replace the Model 2 as that continued on until 1982, although the Model 2 did change to black plastic grips around 1965. SP50 production was carried on by various firms after Milbro/Diana ceased trading and is probably still in production somewhere.

Other firms who may either have manufactured or had pistols marked for them by other firms included Phoenix, Hy-Score, L.J.Cammell, Perfecta and Umarex.

Of these firms Phoenix became Hy-Score, L.J.Cammell was a pellet making firm, (see notes). A Perfecta version of this pistol has not yet been examined. The Umarex Company sells other firms air weapons under their own trademark.

Pistol no. 63, Diana/Milbro SP50 .177 pistol box.

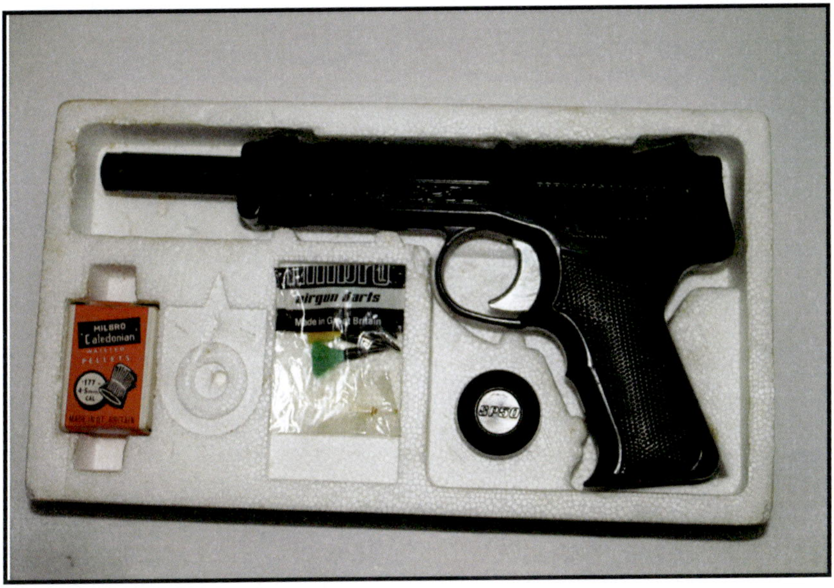

Pistol no. 63, mint boxed Diana SP50.

Pistol no. 63, right side of Diana/Milbro SP50.

Pistol no. 35, left side of Phoenix G50.

Pistol no. 35, right side detail of Phoenix G50.

Pistol no. 35, left side detail of Phoenix G50 safety catch markings.

Pistol no. 61, left side detail of Hy-Score G50.

Pistol no. 61, right side detail of .177 Hy-Score G50.

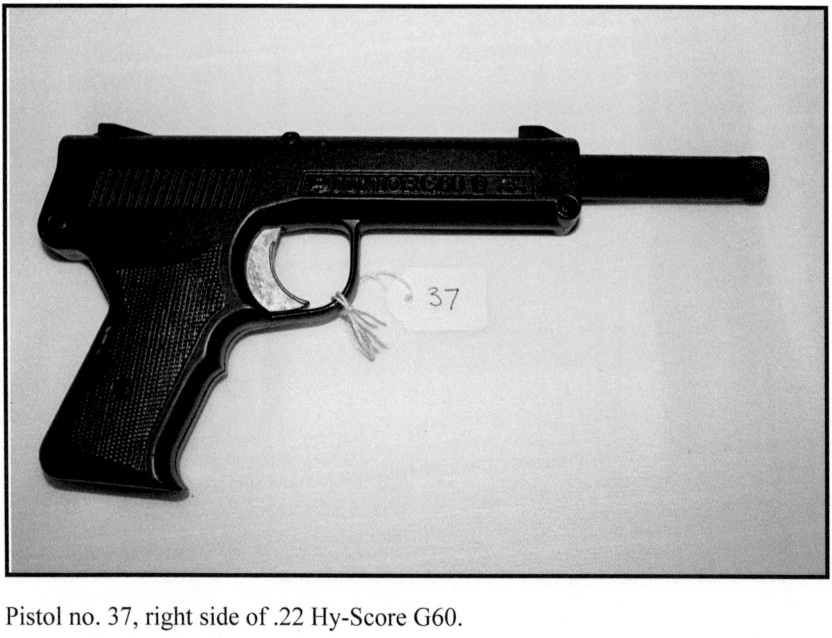

Pistol no. 37, right side of .22 Hy-Score G60.

Pistol no. 37, right side detail of .22 Hy-Score G60.

Pistol no. 37, left side detail of .22 Hy-Score G60.

Pistol no. 37, left side rear detail of .22 Hy-Score G60, note filled safety catch.

Pistol no. 36, right side detail of Champion J.50.

Pistol no. 36, detail of Champion J.50 box.

Pistol no. 36, inner detail of Champion J.50 box, note alloy cocking aid.

Pistol no. 38, right side of chrome plated Umarex SP50 circa 1983 to 2000.

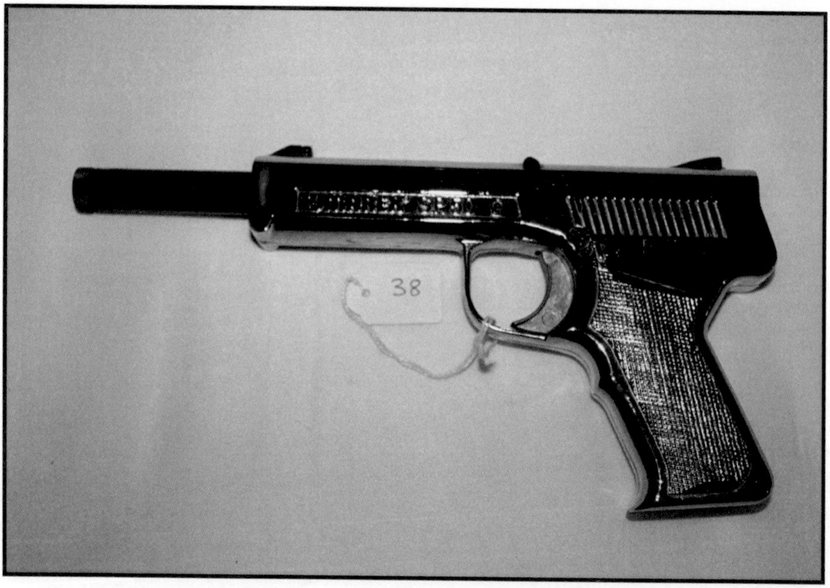

Pistol no. 38, left side of chrome plated Umarex SP50 circa 1983 to 2000.

Pistol no. 38, right side of chrome plated Umarex, showing crosshead screws.

Pistol no. 38, left side of chrome plated Umarex, showing low power mark.

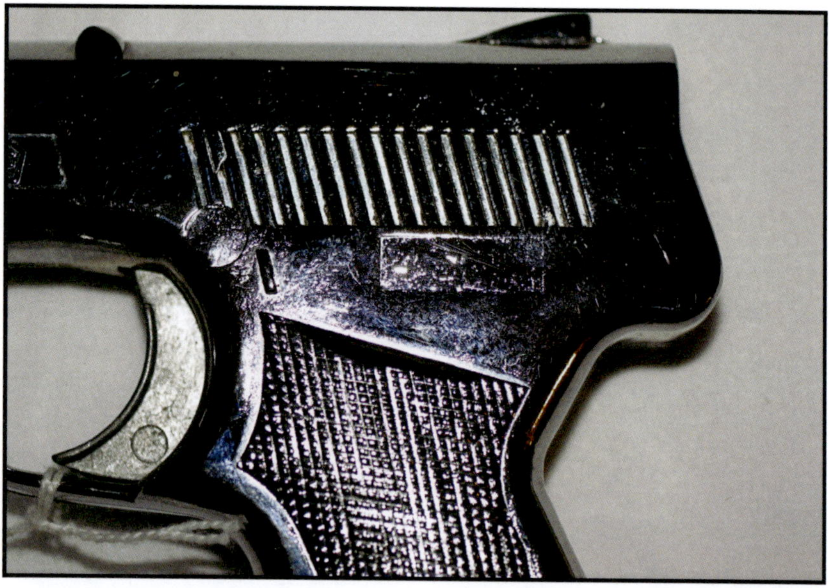

Pistol no. 38, left side of chrome Umarex, showing filled safety & calibre mark.

Pistol no. 38, right side of chrome plated Umarex, showing ground out mark.

Diana SP50 spares list.

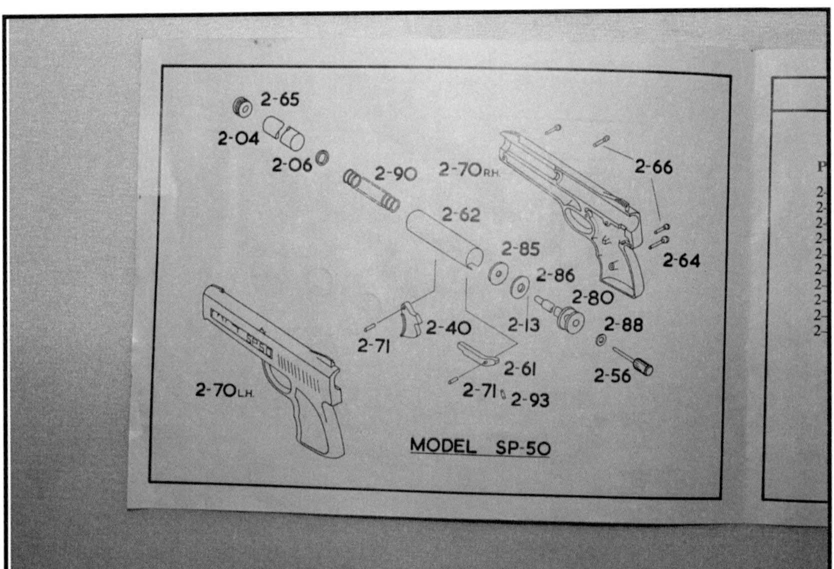

Diana SP50 exploded diagram.

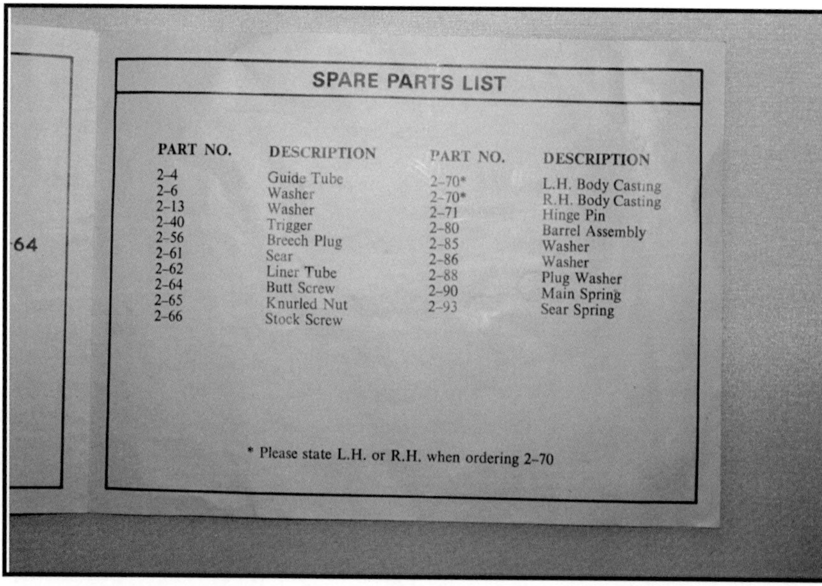

SPARE PARTS LIST

PART NO.	DESCRIPTION	PART NO.	DESCRIPTION
2-4	Guide Tube	2-70*	L.H. Body Casting
2-6	Washer	2-70*	R.H. Body Casting
2-13	Washer	2-71	Hinge Pin
2-40	Trigger	2-80	Barrel Assembly
2-56	Breech Plug	2-85	Washer
2-61	Sear	2-86	Washer
2-62	Liner Tube	2-88	Plug Washer
2-64	Butt Screw	2-90	Main Spring
2-65	Knurled Nut	2-93	Sear Spring
2-66	Stock Screw		

* Please state L.H. or R.H. when ordering 2-70

Diana SP50 spares list.

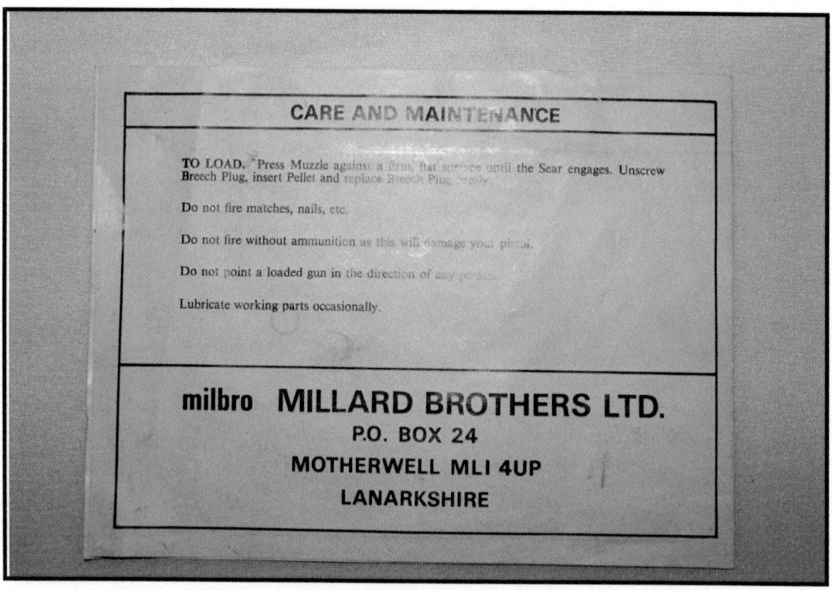

CARE AND MAINTENANCE

TO LOAD. Press Muzzle against a firm, flat surface until the Sear engages. Unscrew Breech Plug, insert Pellet and replace Breech Plug firmly.

Do not fire matches, nails, etc.

Do not fire without ammunition as this will damage your pistol.

Do not point a loaded gun in the direction of any person.

Lubricate working parts occasionally.

milbro MILLARD BROTHERS LTD.
P.O. BOX 24
MOTHERWELL ML1 4UP
LANARKSHIRE

Diana SP50 maintenance instructions.

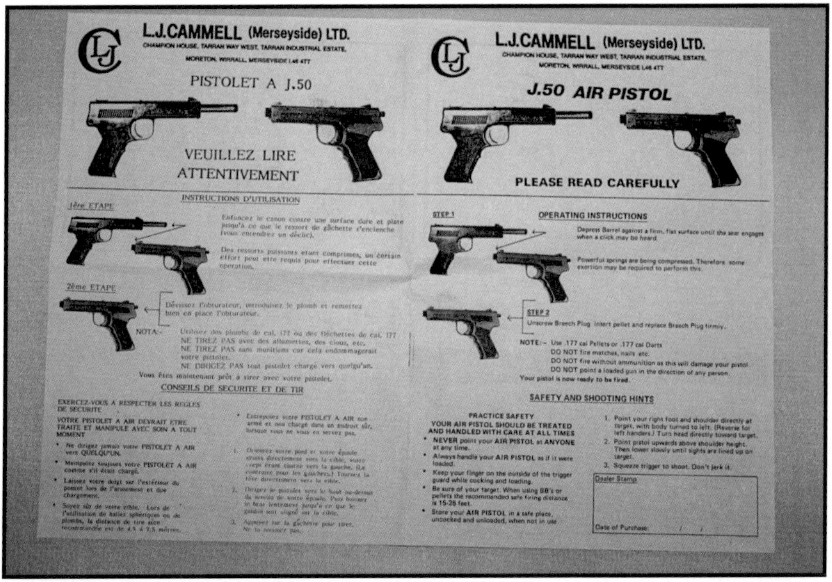

Champion J.50 bi-lingual instruction sheet.

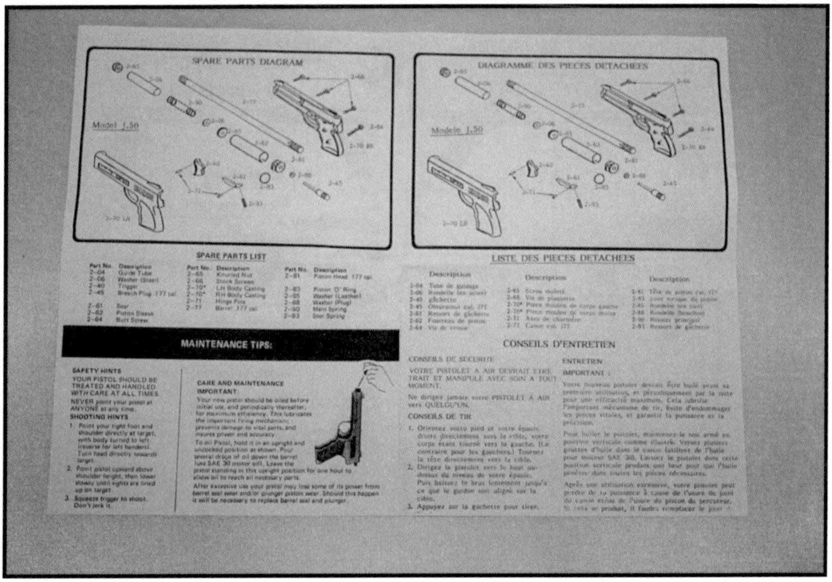

Champion J.50 instruction sheet showing exploded diagram.

Diana SP50 plastic pusher

Box of 100 .177 Caledonian pellets.

Description.

The Diana/Milbro pistols were covered in the preamble to this chapter and were in production from about 1972 till closure of the firm in 1982, the earliest advert found so far was in Guns Review for G.Bate (Gunmakers) Ltd. 16 Colmore Circus, Birmingham, it was not included in the December 1972 advert but by December 1973 it had appeared as the Diana SP50 – NEW, fires pellets, darts .177. £4.95 + 27p. post and packing.

Pistol no. 35, Phoenix Arms Company of Horam, East Sussex may have acquired the rights or possibly machinery following the Milbro closure to make the SP50 as the G50, however the pistol did not appear in either the 1983 or 1984 catalogues and in fact seems not to have been produced until around 1989 to 1990 when it appeared in adverts for Phoenix Arms Co. Ltd. now at Dept. R7, Hy-Score Works, 40 Stonar Road Industrial Estate, Sandwich, Kent. CT13 9LN. The firm appears to have been moving about which might explain the production delays. Anyway by 1990 the pistol was advertised as the Airpower G50, the price had risen to £10.95. Slightly later there was notification that a .22 version was being produced as the G60. Phoenix Arms also acquired production rights in the late 1980's for the American Hy-Score pistol which had been made by the Hy-Score Arms Co. of New York. Following the closure of that firm the English firm started producing a modified version of this pistol around 1990, but the initial advertised price in July 1990 was £65.00 which seems to have been too high as the price was dropped to £59.95 by August. Shortly afterwards the firm started trading as Hy-Score and the G50 appeared with the Hy-Score slide markings.

It is noticeable that most SP50 clones have a filled hole and cast stops on the left side which seem to indicate that a safety catch was to have been fitted at some time but was later omitted. This would place all pistols with these marks as being post 1982. No type 50 pistols with safety catches have been seen.

Pistol no. 61, Hy-Score G50 marked .177, this pistol is estimated to be later than 1993, note the use of Junior on the right side and the addition of the pentagonal F low power marking.

Pistol no. 37, a very rare animal indeed, a .22 gat! the Hy-Score G60, presumably there was also a Phoenix version produced around 1992 but so far no pistol with this marking has emerged, the .22 Hy-Score G60 was probably produced around 1995, the only visible difference between the G50 and G60 are the larger bore and the calibre change on the left side from 4.5mm to .22.

Pistol no. 36, the Champion J.50 produced by L.J.Cammell (Merseyside) Ltd. Champion House, Tarren Way West, Tarren Industrial Estate, Moreton, Wirral, Merseyside. L45 4TT. The date of manufacture is uncertain but is possibly in the late 1990's as can remember buying a batch of unsold receiver stock around 2004 for a unit trade price of £6.95, which was less than half of the retail price. This pistol also has the redundant safety catch markings and was supplied in a substantial white card box with an alloy pusher and the undated instructions in English and French would seem to point to significant sales and exportation to at least France.

Pistol no. 38, produced either for or by Umarex, a company established in both Germany and America as an umbrella organisation selling various other firms air weapons plus others under their own trademark, the Umarex mark was first spotted on a datable pistol when it was found on a Milbro Diana G10 repeater with a mid. 1970's box, the pistol and box were American made and this appears to have been normal with this Milbro pistol. The Umarex mark appeared in very tiny cast letters on the right hand rear of the pistol, Umarex is still in operation and very successful, selling a huge range of items, so we have possible production ranging over thirty five years at least, pistol no. 38 cannot be earlier than 1982 and probably no later than 2000, so estimated it was made around 1996 or possibly later. Unusual as it is chrome plated which is somewhat uncommon, also it shows several alterations under the plating where various markings have been obliterated the most unusual being above the right grip panel where a possible trademark has been removed.

Dimensions.

Overall length. 9 13/16'' 250 mm. Weight. 1lb 8 1/2 oz 694 grm.

Values.

Hopefully from a few pence or a pint of beer to £50+ for mint/boxed. Add a large premium for a .22 and a smaller one for chrome plate.

Auction. £10 and £15. Only black .177's have appeared in auction.

Notes.

A Perfecta G60 version in .22 has been seen and it conforms pretty much to the details of pistol no. 37 except both side panels are marked Perfecta G60 and there is no low power F pentagonal marking.

The firm of L.J.Cammell was operated by Luke Camalleri at that time and as such was responsible for the production of Marksman brand air gun pellets. It is a distinct probability that they were not the actual manufacturers of the Champion pistol but that it was badge engineered for them by one of Diana's later successors.

Dolla Mark II.

In parallel with the cast iron Dolla pistols and originating in the early 1930's there was a blued tinplate Mark II produced up to the start of WWII, unfortunately no sample of this pistol has yet been located, but it would probably bear a strong resemblance to the Super Briton (which see). Post war production probably resumed around 1947 to 1948 and manufacture of the wooden grip version was undertaken by J.G.Anschutz of West Germany, the wood grip lasted until around 1954, when a modernised, black gripped version was issued as the J.G.A. pistol.

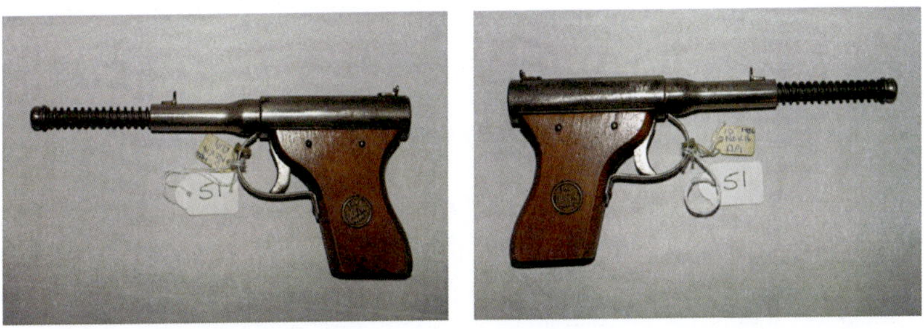

Pistol no. 51, left and right side view, showing brass Dolla medallion each side.

Close up of brass inset Dolla badge in left grip.

The tinplate versions were available in black, presumably also in a nickel or possibly chrome finish, although there is no definitive proof of this. The wooden grip versions have been seen as both blue and chrome, the wood grip finish also varies from pale brown to a reddish colour with both matt and gloss varnishes. There is insufficient data as yet to see if the varying grip colour could be an aid toward dating these pistols.

Dimensions.

Overall length. 8 1/16'' 205mm. Weight. 9 3/4 oz 274 grm.

Values.

Something of a hard one to value, wood grip version probably £25 to £100, probably double for a boxed mint example. Tinplate one is much rarer.

Auction. £250, only price seen for a wood grip version but either it was factory fresh, mint and boxed or two or more people were very, very desperate to buy it.

Notes.

German Diana Model 2's.

Meyer and Grammelspacher of Rastatt, Germany, the company that would eventually manufacture Diana airguns started in the mid 1890's making air rifles and pistols under the MGR trademark. The first pistol appears to have been a cast iron quasi gat type, loaded with a pusher pin into the static barrel but with a pull down rod which cocked a cylinder contained within the butt using a separate cocking tool. The trademark MGR was cast into the floral pattern above the trigger and may not be obvious on examples with worn paint or plating. Also sold as the Tahiti by A.W.Gamage, during the Edwardian period.

In 1925, following on from the cast iron pistol, the firm which since 1905 had been using the Diana trademark then turned to producing tinplate pistols. The first tinplate pistol was a continuation of the butt cocking cast pistol but the gat type barrel was replaced by a pull forward and drop barrel, this was known as the Model 1 and was in production until around 1935, although advertising carried on for quite a long while afterwards.

During the early 1930's and possibly alongside the Model 1, production of the Model 2 commenced. This was a genuine gat type push in barrel cocker with a pusher pin to position the pellet or dart within the concentric barrel, earliest pistols were most probably the ribbed grip versions as these would have been similar to the grips on the Model 1. However this soon changed around the mid 30's to smooth grip panels with the Diana huntress design each side with the word Diana in the rectangular panel above it, some of these pistols have Made in Germany in small script down the front edge of the grip. Around 1937 the huntress moved to the top of the cylinder with a small Mod 2 beneath and tiny Made in Germany beneath that leaving a plain lower grip. Apparently just prior to the outbreak of WW2 the wooden grip versions appeared, production continued throughout the war until 1945. Post war German production of weapons was banned totally and Diana's machinery was dismantled, (see the British G2 section for details). However following the relaxation of the ban in the late 40's, by 1950 Diana was back in production suggesting that not all of the machinery had been seized as war reparations. However Diana was forced due to the loss of its trademark to use other trademarks especially when dealing with Britain and most probably the Commonwealth countries. Alternate marks included Original, Original Diana, Milbro Foreign and others. There was a lot of pre-war interaction between Diana and Milbro and possibly post war as well.

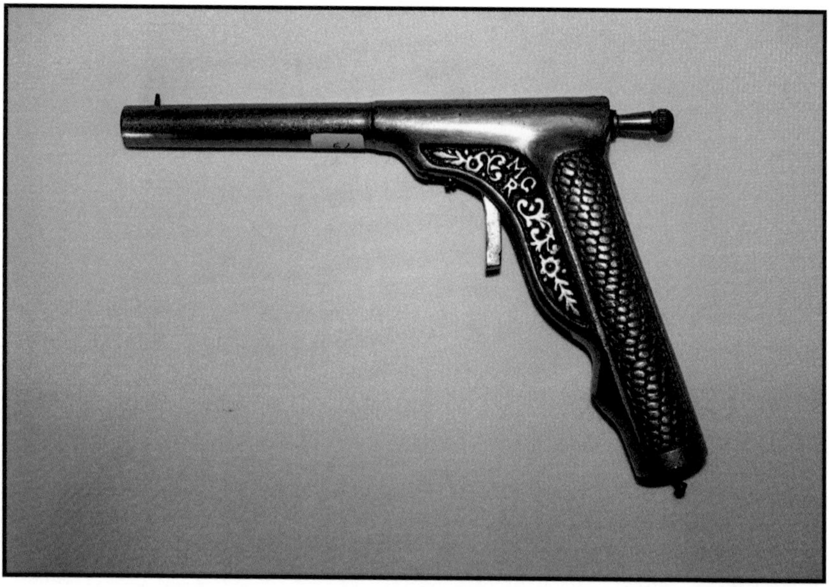

Pistol no. 79, nickelled cast iron, earliest type of pistol produced by M.G.R.

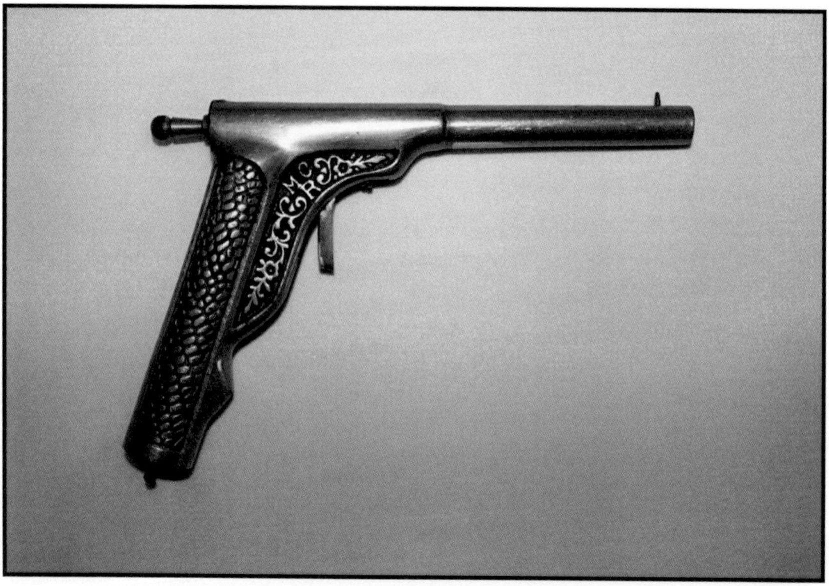

Pistol no.79, cocking rod in butt, pellet pusher as per gat type pistols.

Pistol no. 79, M.G.R. trademark cast into foliage above trigger

Pistol no. 72, Model 1, right side, un-cocked with barrel open ci. 1930.

Pistol no. 72, Model 1, left side, pistol in fired position.

Pistol no. 16, right side, showing huntress, unfortunately in relic order ci. 1935

Pistol no. 54, right side, showing huntress trademark, ci. 1935.

Pistol no. 54, left side, showing huntress trademark, ci. 1935.

Pistol no. 54, Made in Germany stamping on front of grip.

Pistol no. 52, Made in Germany stamping on front of grip.

Pistol no. 52, nickel or chrome plate, right side ci.1935.

Pistol no. 52, nickel or chrome plate, left side ci.1935.

Pistol no. 53, showing plain grip panel, estimated date 1937.

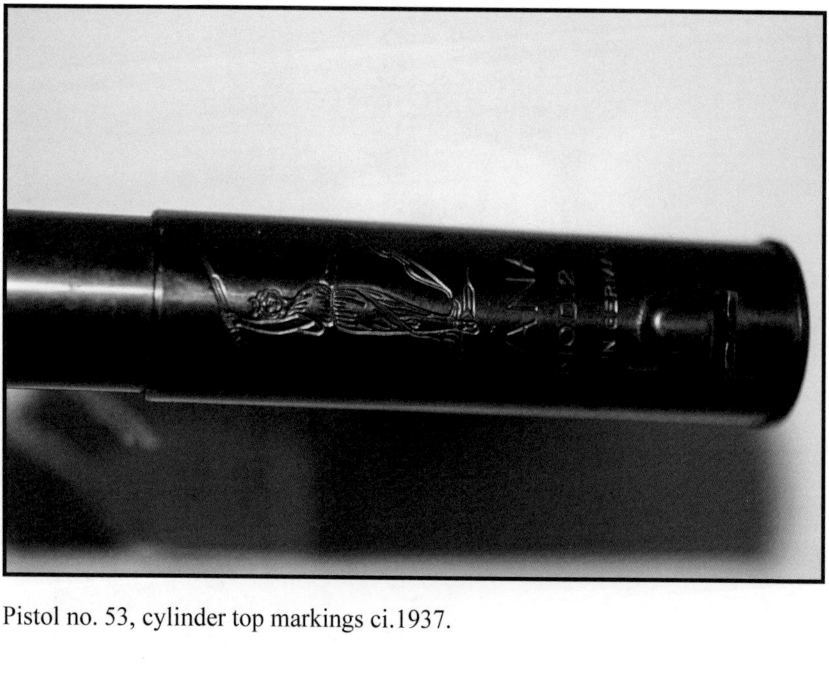

Pistol no. 53, cylinder top markings ci.1937.

Pistol no. 67, right side, wooden gripped, estimated date 1937 to 1945.

Pistol no. 67, left side, wood gripped, estimated date 1937 to 1945.

Pistol no. 67, cylinder top markings, wooden gripped.

Pistol no. 73, pre-war Swedish contract ?.

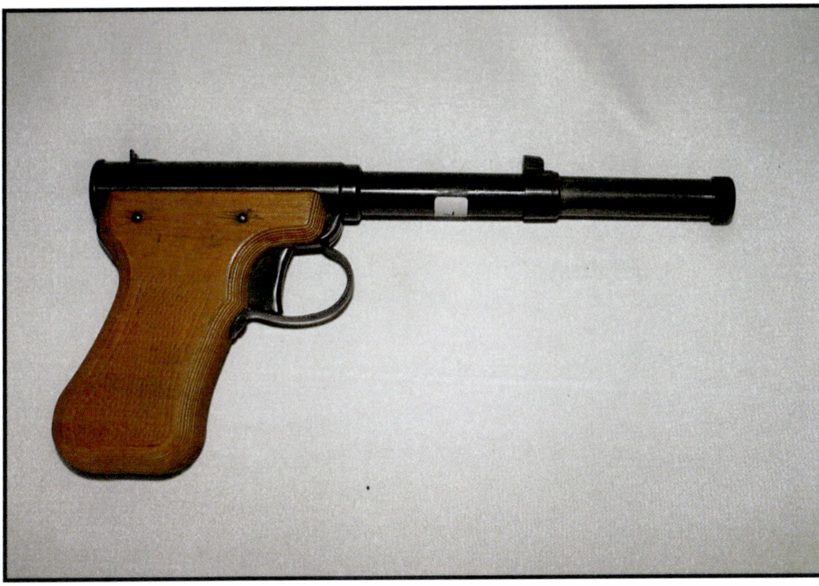

Pistol no. 73, has modernised grip but is much thinner than normal production.

Pistol no. 49, right side, post war Original with modified grip shaping ci. 1952.

Pistol no. 49, left side, post war Original with modified grip shaping ci. 1952.

Pistol no. 49, cylinder top markings, old label states 1952 but possibly later.

Pistol no. 49, tiny marking on left side of cylinder.

Pistol no. 84, very similar to no. 49 except for left side cylinder markings.

Pistol no. 84, post war markings circa 1955, must be later than no. 49.

Descriptions.

Unfortunately no pre-war German examples of the early rib grip pistols were available for examination however an early wood grip pistol which may prove to be German made can be found as pistol no. 31 in the British Diana chapter.

It is noticeable that all post 1925 German made or marked pistols, including those made pre-war appear to be fitted with crescent curved triggers.

Pistol no. 79, M.G.R. circa 1900, nickel plated cast iron with an inserted brass barrel, operated by pulling down on the cocking rod in the butt, in this case using a separate tool. Other pistols possibly of later manufacture had nicely shaped tee handles permanently attached to the rod. Loaded via a gat type pusher pin directly into the end of the fixed barrel. Production life was from around 1895 to 1925 and the pistol was produced in fairly large numbers in either nickel or black enamel finishes. This represented the first type of pistol produced by Meyer and Grammelspacher and was very well made. Supplied in a simple wooden box with a few pellets, darts and targets.

Pistol no. 72, Model 1 tinplate Diana, blued finish, although this pistol has a tinplate outer skin there is significant amount of solid steel and machined parts contained inside, it is quite a heavy and tallish pistol. Due to the cocking tool being separate and therefore easily lost these pistols are often found with bars or rings welded, usually very badly to the cocking rod. Probably too expensive for a cheap pistol and was superseded by the Model 2. Made in Germany, stamped on front edge of grip. Many years ago saw one in a bright nickel finish.

Pistol no. 16, early pre-war blued pistol circa 1935, unfortunately the pistol is in relic order but shows the Huntress trademark on the grips with the word Diana in the rectangle above each grip, foresight missing from this sample but was of the inserted type.

Pistol no. 54, blued, details much as pistol no. 16 but with the addition of the words Made in Germany in small lettering down the front of the grip, again circa 1935 but suspect of later manufacture than pistol no. 16.

Pistol no. 52, nickel plated with the same markings and of approximately of the same date as pistol no. 54.

Pistol no. 53, blued with plain grip panels, the Huntress trademark has moved to the top of the cylinder with Mod 2 below and Made in Germany in small lettering beneath, estimated date circa 1937.

Pistol no. 67, blued with wooden grip, markings as pistol no. 53, estimated to be circa 1937 to possibly 1945.

Pistol no. 73, purchased after no. 49, this one really throws a spanner in the works, sold via auction as pre-war or wartime production for a Swedish contract, it has some attributes which may point toward British post 1952 production. OK, it may well have been made for a Swedish contract but unlike the post war Original it has a much thinner butt than normal post war production, the blued securing pins protrude about 1mm each side, also fitted with a re-curved trigger. Was this produced covertly by Milbro for Diana?

Pistol no. 49, M & G post war production made in approximately 1952 with the modernized and certainly better shaped wooden grips, Original in script with mod 2 beneath on cylinder top. This pistol appears to break with the idea that all German pistols were fitted with crescent curved triggers as this gun appears to be fitted with a re-curved trigger. (see no. 73) possibly made by Milbro which would explain the trigger. Sold in U.S. as the Hy-Score Model 814 Junior.

Pistol no. 84, a blued pistol, with modernized chequered light wooden grip. Very similar to no. 49 except for the differing wording of the tiny lettering above the left grip which changes from Made in Germany to Made in West Germany. The root cause of the change was the hardening Soviet post war response leading to the eventual erection of the Berlin Wall. In 1949 the Western allies had founded the Federal Republic of Germany which soon became better known by the alternate name of West Germany. Following the successful Berlin airlift Russian attitude hardened and what had been reasonable access between East and West was quickly curtailed by increasing Soviet security measures which culminated in the building of the actual concrete wall in the early 1950's, this pistol probably dates from around 1955 to circa 1965.

Dimensions.

Cast iron M.G.R.

Overall length. 8'' 203mm. Weight. 1lb 3 7/8 oz 563 grm.

Model 1

Overall length. 8 1/16'' 205mm. Weight. 1lb 3 3/8 oz 555 grm.

Model 2 Average of several pistols.

Overall length. 9 7/8'' 251mm. Weight. 11 3/8 oz 325 grm.

Values.

Value. MGR cast iron £250 to £700.

Auction. MGR cast iron £550.

Value. Model 1 tinplate £25 to £150

Auction. Model 1 tinplate not seen as separate item.

Value. Pre-war tinplate £15 to £100.

Auction. Pre-war tinplate £25, £70, £80.

Value. Post-war £5 to £40.

Auction. Post-war £10, £5, £15, £12 & £15.

Harrington Gats.

Manufactured by T.J.Harrington & Sons Limited of Magda Works Trading Estate, Moseley Road, Walton, Surrey.

This firm appeared to have some connection with either the production of or more likely the retailing of a early to late 1930's tinplate pistol called the GARANTA, an apparent clone of the German tinplate Diana Model 2, the only obvious differences were the chequered upper grip panel rectangles and the lower panels which were plain with a pressed out *Garanta* in italic script at an angle across them. Just pre or more likely post war saw the production of the die cast versions, the manufacture of which carried on until around 2000 when Gat production rights were transferred to Marksman Products USA and others following the death of James Harrington in 1996.

The post-war die-cast Gat is one of the toughest and probably the most common British gats to be found, it is also the most versatile being mostly fitted with the built in cork holder which allowed it to be used with a wide variety of ammunition, many types of which did not fall into the usual range of projectiles.

Four main variations were made, Early Type 1 without corkholder and with separate grips, Type 2 prior to introduction of the safety catch, Type 3, a short lived version with contoured grip and small figure safety catch and the Type 4 with large figure safety catch, altered grip and lighter rear cylinder reinforce.

After examining a fairly large cross section of Gat's and copious amounts of magazines and catalogues, it was apparent that there was very little advertising, in fact in a 30 year period I only managed to find two adverts. However, Alan Harvey pointed out that I was looking in the wrong place, most of the advertising appearing in the Scout, Boys Own, Meccano and similar magazines, not the shooting press.

There appeared to be no obvious way to date Gat's, purchase dates were not much use beyond establishing the latest date at which a certain variation was sold. Black pistols were much cheaper than the chrome ones and were probably outselling them by about 5 to 1 and unlike Webley pistols which came in ones and twos into Bosleys, (our local emporium), Gats were ordered in batches and stacked on the back shelves with the inevitable mixing of variations, not helped by being in similar type boxes for a long period.

To try and establish a dating scale it was obvious that a different approach was needed, two methods were tried, one involving the varying markings and another which did not become obvious until several Gats had been examined, when it was noted that there was a great variation in the cork holders.

Gat muzzle nut/cork holders

Type CH1

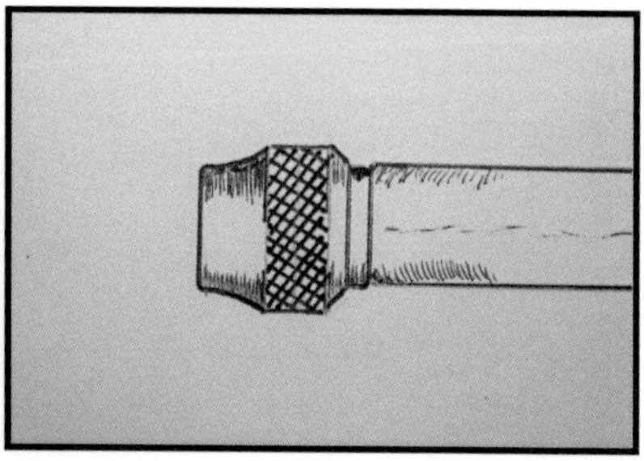

Type CH2

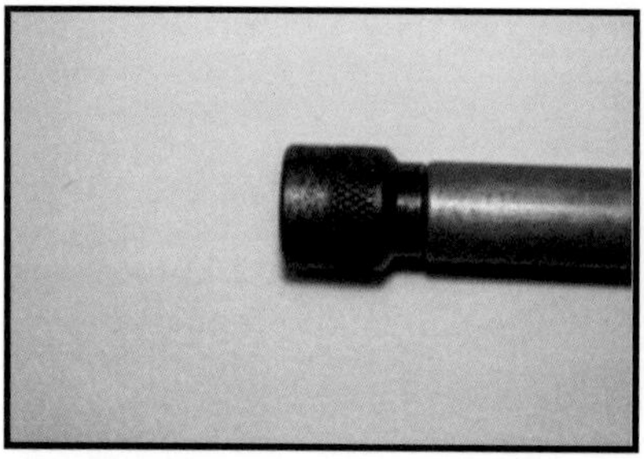

Type CH3

Type CH4

Type CH5

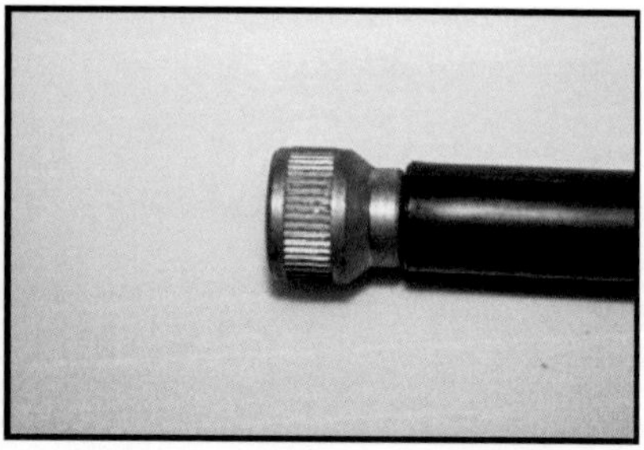

Type CH6

Gat muzzle nut/cork holders.

Type CH7

Type CH8

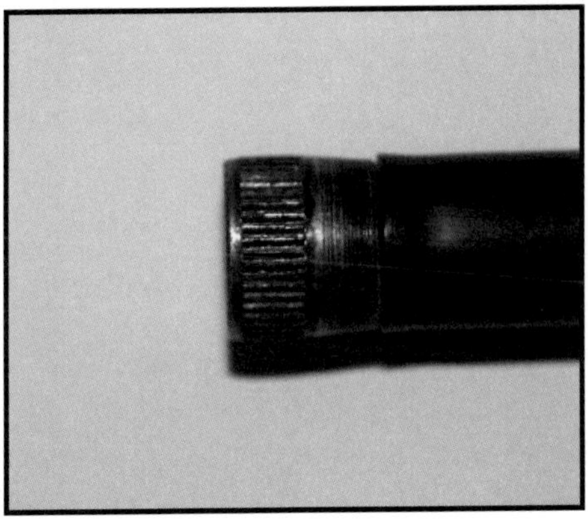

Type CH9

Descriptions of Corkholders.

Type CH1, very early pre or more likely just post war Type 1 Gat (pistol no.1) without cork holder, muzzle nut 0.25in. (6mm) deep, chequered. Date estimated as 1939 to 1948 which excludes the war and probably 1946 due to early post war material shortages. Pistol no.1 also disproved the theory that the patent applied for markings on these pistols refers to the corkholder, as no.1 has an ordinary muzzle nut but is still marked patent, so that is one theory right out of the window. It is possible that the patent may refers to methods of die casting or may even be of a spurious nature, further research is definitely needed.

Descriptions of Corkholders.

Type CH2, as Type CH3 but with the forward portion of the corkholder reduced down to a smaller diameter, chequered band in same rearward position, known on a Type 2 pistol circa 1952 and in 1958 book illustration. Corkholder 0.79in. (20mm).

Type CH3, on Type 2 pistol no.2, straight portion in front of chequered band, noted in literature as post 1958. Corkholder 0.79in. (20mm).

Type CH4, Finer chequering moved slightly more towards muzzle, Type 2 pistol no.3 had an old label stating 1985. Corkholder 0.79in. (20mm).

Type CH5, Chequered band now central in cylindrical portion of the corkholder, but overall length shortened to 0.67in. (17mm) Type 2 pistol.

Type CH6, Chequered pattern changed to a heavy rolled bar pattern, overall length 0.67in. (17mm).

Type CH 7, possibly only a result of wear in the tooling, but the bar pattern appears lighter; the length has been shortened once again to 0.59in. (15mm). This type of corkholder appears to have been produced when the Gat design was modernized to the new contour grip and safety catch model. New shape Type 3 pistol no.12 was purchased on the 22/10/1994 for £13.75, in the new type cellophane fronted box, complete with darts, pellets and corks.

Type CH8, very similar to Type CH7 except shortened by 1mm. to 0.55in. (14mm), appears to coincide with the modified and reshaped Type 4 pistol.

Type CH9 special shape corkholder fitted to Gat air rifle with strengthened rear.

Gat Markings. Right Side (R).

All Gats carry clear markings on both sides of the pistol, however, there is a distinct series of changes that can be placed in order of appearance, note some markings on one side may stay the same while the other side changes so both sides need to be examined to find out where a particular pistol will fit in the series. Markings are taken as either Right (R) or Left (L) looking from the rear of the pistol. Also noted an internet description of what must have been a late pistol which carried the four line safety poem, but on which side was not clear.

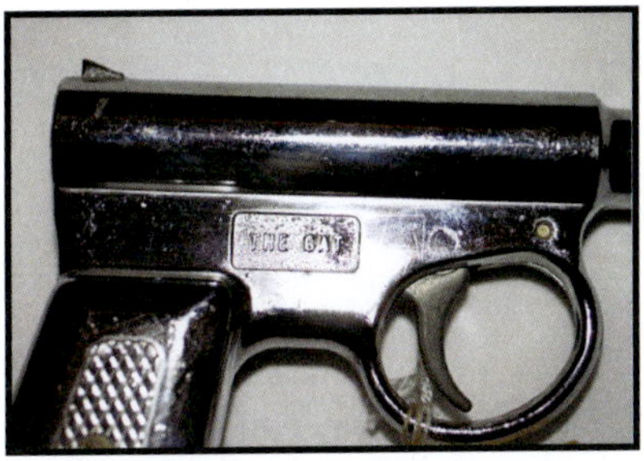

Type R1on earliest known Type 1 Gat.

Type R1 early production Type 2.

Type R1 later production Type 2.

Type R2 no stippling

Type R3

Type R4

Type R5, note low power ‘F’marking.

Description of Right Side Markings.

R1. This marking appears from the earliest known Type 1 pistol and carried on with various slight differences of stippling and edging through most of the production life of the Type 2 pistols, the stippling gradually getting lighter until it disappeared altogether.

R2. Appearing on very late Type 2 pistols, as R1, but minus stippling.

R3. Manufactured by or for Umarex with the European derived low power marking of a pentagonal enclosed F, this means Type 3 pistols must be post 1972 as that was when legislation relating to this marking was introduced.

R4. As R3, but with the addition of the calibre marking 4.5mm.

R5. Manufactured by or for a so far unknown company but has 4.5mm calibre marking and is a Type 4 pistol so appears to be later than R4.

Gat Markings. Left Side (L).

Type L1

Type L2

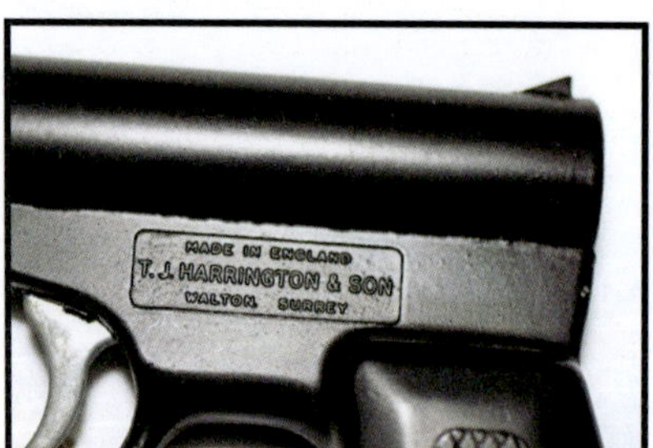

Type L3

Type L4

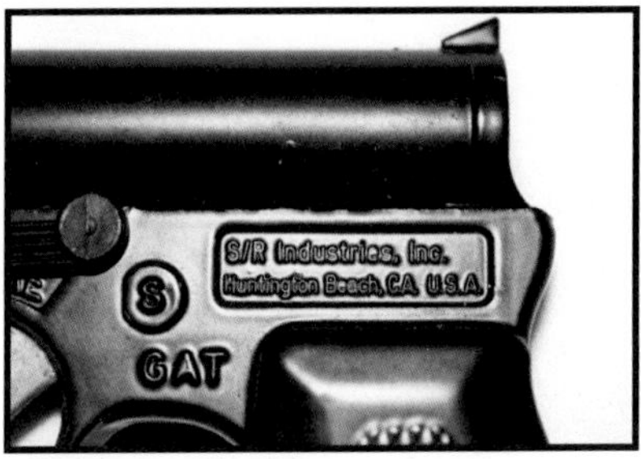

Type L5.

Description of Left side markings.

L1, T.J.H & Son, deep stamping with stippling on earliest known Type 1 pistol.

L2, T.J.H & Son, shallower edge to stamping, stippled background. Normal marking for Type 2 pistols. Stippling appears to have become lighter as manufacture proceeded until on later pistols it disappears.

L3, T.J.Harrington & Son, marking found on very late Type 2 pistols and possibly on very early Type 3 modernized pistols, although the stamping line spacing did vary on the L4 markings.

L4, variation of L3, marking was moved towards the rear of the Type 3 pistol, stamping noticeably cruder than previously, may also occur on early Type 4 pistols.

L5, T.J.Harrington & Son markings can also be found in this position, where the stamp has remained static but the grip shape has been altered to the later Type 4 specification, the stamping shown relates to late manufacture by or for S.R.Industries USA.

Safety Catch Markings

Type SC1 on Type 3 pistol.

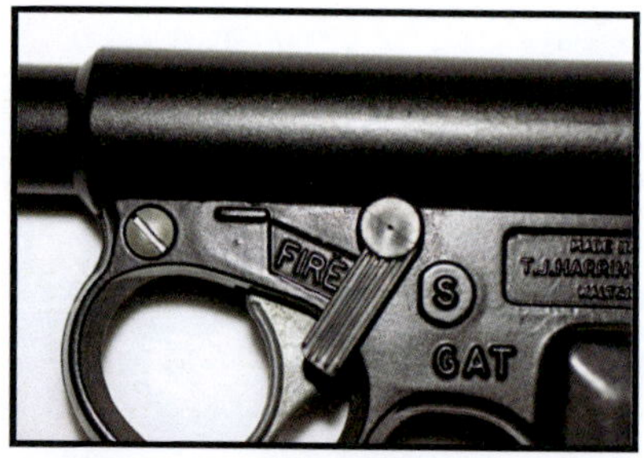

Type SC2 on Type 4 pistol.

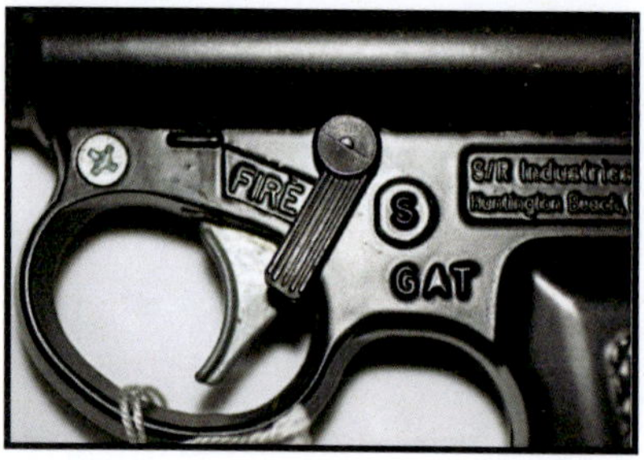

Type SC3 on Type 4 pistol. (Late).

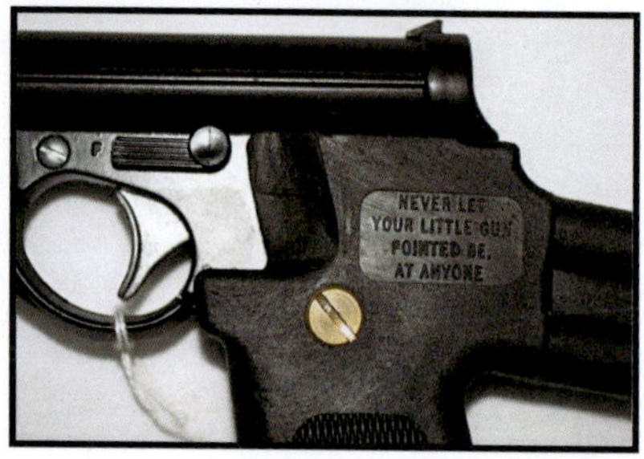

Type SC4 Gat Air Rifle

Description of Safety Catch markings.

Apparently safety catches were introduced circa 1982 to cater for American market demands, however given the trigger pull required to fire a Gat, the safety catch fitting was probably about as useful as a chocolate teapot.

It is possible that the red trigger seen on pistol no. 6 was a very early attempt at a visible safety warning, it certainly is an uncommon variation and would seem to fall into about the correct time frame. Safety catches have only been seen on Type 3 & 4 modernized shape pistols, however it is not beyond the realms of possibility that a few very late Type 2 pistols may have been fitted with catches, also there may well have been a crossover of markings when the Type 3 pistols were superseded by the Type 4. Differences between the two types can be seen on the Type 4 by the squaring off of the front top of the grip and the much thinner reinforcement on the rear end of the cylinder.

Description of Safety Catch markings.

SC1. Early Type 3 pistol with small lettering to safety catch, rounded top front of grip and heavy cylinder reinforce, T.J.Harrington & Son marking.

SC2. Type 4 pistol heavy lettering to safety catch, squared top front to grip and lighter cylinder reinforce, T.J.Harrington & Son marking.

SC3. Type 4 pistol heavy lettering to safety catch, squared top front to grip and lighter cylinder reinforce, S.R.Industries marking, note the use of crosshead fixing screws making this a very late pistol.

SC4. Specific only to the short lived Gat rifle which started production in 1987, although the rifle had a completely different frame arrangement to the pistols the general characteristics were similar to the Type 3 and it was probably produced in parallel with them, it may well have continued production into the Type 4 period.

Catalogue information.

A Henry Krank catalogue circa 1996 to 1997 shows as no. 5243 a Gat rifle and above it no. 5240 a Type 4 Gat pistol with R5 markings.

In the attached price list there is a significant piece of information which confirms a suspicion that I have had for some time. (see notes).

5240 Gat Pistol (in display box)	£13.65
5241 Gat Pistol only (presume this was sold in the soft box)	£11.50
5243 Gat Rifle	£25.50

Unfortunately, there is no illustration of the presumed pistol only box. I certainly cannot remember any separate type 3 and 4 pistols passing through the gun shops that I worked in or visited in the 1980's and up to the late 90's, all of the type 3 and 4 pistols I saw were sold in the clear fronted display box sets with the associated accessories.

Prices seen elsewhere, gives prices around the 1970's as black pistols at 24/- (£1.20p), chrome at 31/-6d (£1.58p) and darts at 2/- (10p) a dozen.

Pistol no. 1, circa 1939 to1947 Type 1 Gat.

Pistol no. 3, Post 1973 Type 2 Gat.

Pistol no. 6, with red trigger, note small British Standard mark underneath boss.

Pistol no. 6, close up of red trigger and tiny BS1004 mark under screw boss.

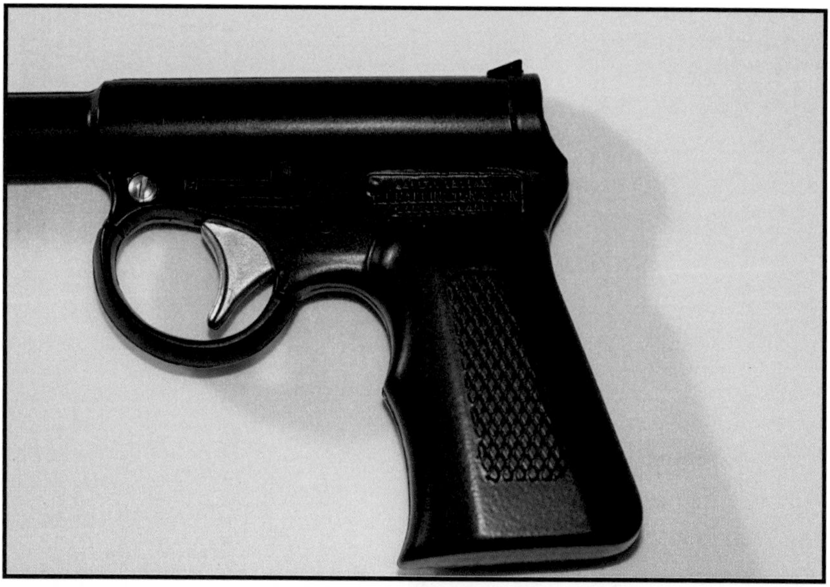

Type 3 Gat, chroming appears to stop with the modernized Types 3 and 4.

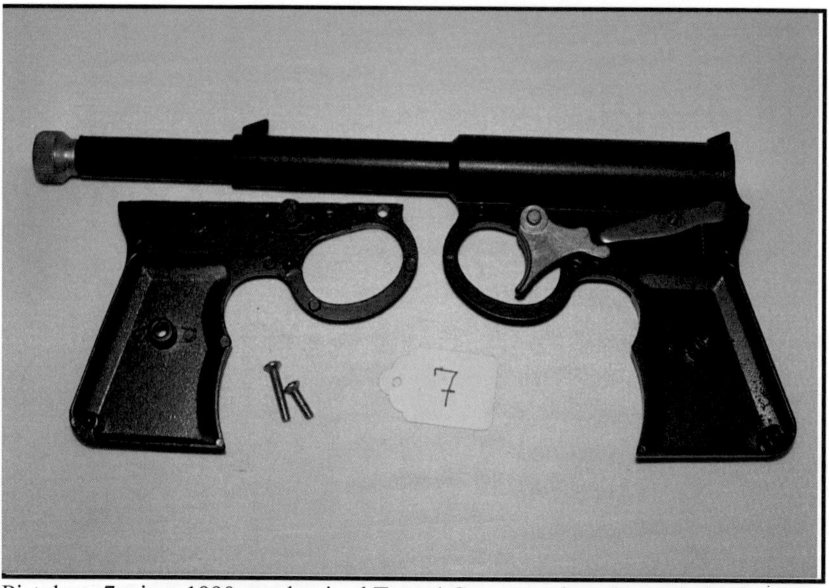

Pistol no. 7, circa 1990, modernized Type 4 Gat, note altered rear limb of trigger to accommodate the safety catch.

Gat Boxes.

Sadly, I have been unable to locate any of the early green boxes with the Indian throwing away his bow on the back (a clear near copy of the Diana logo!), however from personal recollection I know that Type 2 pistols were available in the standard soft card boxes certainly from the late 50's until the change to the modernized safety catch type pistols and even these were sold in soft boxes if purchased separately without accessories.

Box colours were pale blue / black for black pistols and red / black for the chrome/polished versions, with slight variations during production of the Type 2 pistols. However when the first of the Type 3 early modified pistols appeared they were issued (probably only for a short time) in the blue soft card box but there were significant changes to the box front, in comparison with the early box illustrated the no. 1 bore changed to 4.5mm, the pistol drawing was modified to include a safety catch and in the top right hand corner of the box a coloured Union flag appeared. However, very shortly the cellophane fronted box appeared for Type 3 and 4 pistols, this gave a bonus to the air-gunner in the form of a small pot of pellets, five corks, ten darts and two targets on the back of the pack, but a circa 1996 catalogue shows pistols as still being available either in this kit or on their own, in the earlier soft box.

Circa 1960's to 70's box for 2nd type Gat, black, pre safety catch.

Back of Type 2 Gat box.

Later Type 3 and Type 4 box, shown with Type 3 pistol.

Rear of late Type 3 and Type 4 box.

Odd variations.

A black Type 2 pistol was found which had no obvious external differences from normal, on the spur of the moment it was stripped down and found to be a bit of an odd variation as it was fitted with a Type 3 trigger top bar although the trigger was still of the thin blade type, Type 3 triggers are not fitted with the top limb which goes above the sear bar and are normally only fitted to a pistol with a safety catch. There was no sign that the pistol in question had any modifications that would allow a catch to be fitted. It is more than likely that this was a late model Type 2 pistol fitted with an interim type trigger which was quickly superseded by the wider bladed trigger of the Type 3 pistol.

Pistol no.6, is fitted with the red trigger which may have been an early safety warning device, this would place the pistol as post 1982 when American safety legislation was passed, however the inside of the grip has a cast in British Standard BS1004 marking. These markings were the result of legislation passed on 14th September 1972, BS1004 being a specification for zinc alloys and zinc alloy die-casting, specification replaced by BSEN 12844 in 1998 but the use of BS marks appears to have been discontinued some years previously.

Sample Gats in estimated date order.

Pistol	Type	Finish	C/holder	Right	Left	Safety	Slider	Screw
1	1	Chrome	1	R1	L1	-	Chrome	Slot
2	2	Black	3	R1	L2	-	Alloy	Slot
9	2	Black	4	R1	L2	-	Alloy	Slot
32	2	Black	5	R1	L2	-	Alloy	Slot
3	2	Chrome	5	R1	L3	-	Alloy	Slot
59	2	Black	6	R1	L3	-	PVC	Slot
6	2	Chrome	6	R1	L3	-	PVC	Slot
10	3	Black	7	R4	L4	SC1	PVC	Slot
12	3	Black	7	R5	L4	SC1	PVC	Slot
7	4	Black	8	R5	L4	SC2	PVC	Slot*
8	4	Black	8	R5	L5	SC3	PVC	Cross*

Comments

Pistol no.		
	1	Estimated to be circa 1947 with separate grip panels.
	2	Post 1958
	9	Old type blue & black box
	32	Heavy filing of cylinder top moulded seam
	3	Old label states 1985 (?)
	6	Chrome with red trigger, safety related? BS1004 mark
	10	Type 3 in damaged cellophane fronted box
	12	Purchased 22/11/1994, mint & unused
	7	Low power mark, grip slot screw* moved to left grip
	8	Low power mark, grip crosshead screw* moved to left grip

Gat Rifle markings.

The Gat rifle and the associated modernised pistols were a brave effort to re-energise what had become a very dated design. Perhaps a gold plated 50th anniversary collector edition in a wooden box would have had more success. It is so very easy to be wise after the event, but the increasing age restrictions and the vast and rapid improvements in air weapons following the restrictions on handguns especially in Britain meant there was a dearth of junior shooters and those did exist were not able to have access to pistols such as the Gat. Air gunners now wanted accurate weapons and had the disposable income to afford them, hence air weapons at a price and level of complexity which was unthinkable a decade previously, likewise the relaxation on the sale of CO^2 pistols in Britain brought about huge increases in CO^2 sales and tended to overshadow the poor old Gat, it is noticeable that there are very few of the push in barrel type pistols available nowadays.

Gat rifle no.58, right side of rifle showing address and cryptic 1920 embossed on frame side. Frame appears to be alloy with what looks to be a glass reinforced plastic butt, fore-stock appears to be of black pvc type plastic.

Right side butt and fore-grip, with cryptic embossing of No. 1.J.1920.

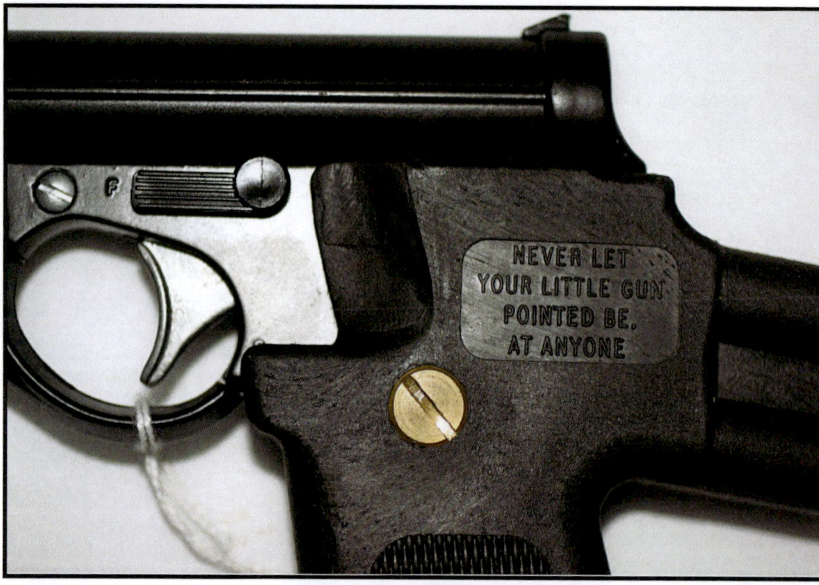

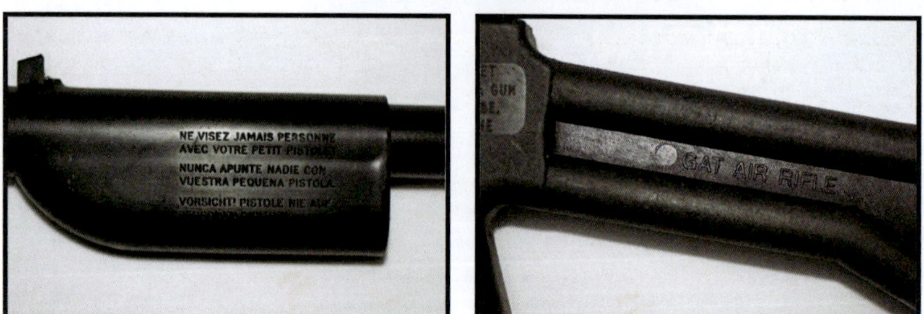

Gat rifle no. 58, left side of rifle showing safety messages in four languages.

Gat Accessories.

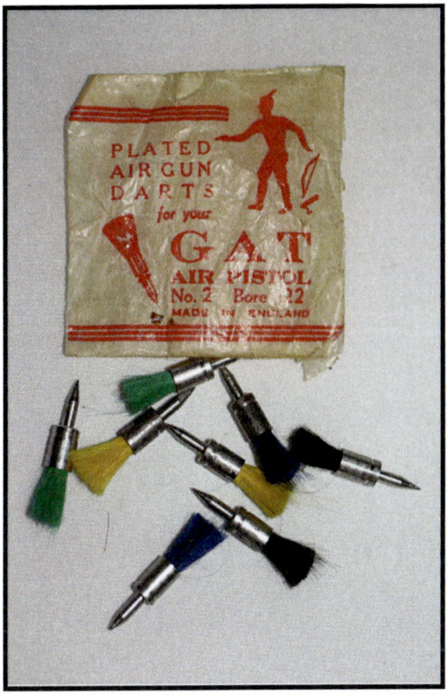

Early Gat? .22 darts.

Accessory pack.

Darts.

The .177 Gat darts were commonplace in the 1960's and many a dartboard, playing card and cardboard box became the targets, but I had these in my ammunition collection for over 40 years but up till recently I had never seen a Gat in anything other than .177, that is until I found a Hy-Score G60 (SP50 clone) which actually was in .22. Note the early Harrington Indian trademark which would appear to place these darts in the early post war period.

Accessories.

The accessory pack was brought out sometime in the late 1980's early 90's, the pistol shown is a safety catch Type 3 or 4 and appears to be firing one of the short lived plastic cruciform flight darts, the pack contains 10 darts, 10 corks, a pack of pellets and a yellow plastic fly swat, (an item that reappears in late packaged American market sets along with a nicely made alloy ramrod). This is an uncommon accessory especially when found unopened.

Pellet boxes.

The small round pvc pellet boxes supplied in the pistol packs have been seen with various coloured bases including clear, red, green and black, most contain standard ribbed diabalo round nosed pellets but a black based box from a very late type 4 pistol kit contained red painted or varnished, flat nose smooth skirted target pellets, very similar to the RWS type.

Advert.

Page from Joseph Bourne and Son 1933 catalogue, showing Garanta pistol.

Dimensions.

Average length. 10 5/8" 271mm. Weight. 1lb 2 1/4oz 521 grm.

An average length and weight has been given for Gats as there are many slight variations in the dimensions across the range of the four variations of pistol.

Values.

The Gat pistol was available in at least three finishes.

Black, which was the most common finish, note, there are some obvious manufacturing variations in the types of paint finish.

Chrome, rarer than the black version and would attract a slight premium, but the finish is more durable than the black and is often found in better condition.

Polished, also available for a short period around the 1960's in a polished finish, it may be that this finish was a result of the chrome shortages or an attempt to cut costs, apparently supplied in a soft red/black box with the word chrome on the front replaced by the word polished. A word of warning, it would be very easy to polish up a tatty black pistol to this specification. Rare, probably worth at least double the price of a normal pistol especially if boxed.

Condition is the arbiter of price, followed by any rare variations that may be found, however even the rarest Gat is unlikely to break the bank, boxed sets do up the price especially on American e Bay (load-sa-money) but in Britain most Gats can be purchased for £5 to £25, slightly more for the soft box and about £40 to £60 for a minter in a later window type box with all the fittings. The darts and accessory pack could be almost any price from 50p upwards for the darts and up to £10 for the pack.

Auction prices are an estimate as these pistols seldom appear singly, most often found in job lots with other pistols. Estimated prices at around £3 to £20.

Notes.

Details of the polished Gats can be found in Dennis. E. Hilliers most excellent 3rd edition of the Collectors Guide to Airpistols (1993). Details of a very late box were discovered, it contained a late type 4 pistol with crosshead screws, it was similar to the type 3, type 4 box illustrated, however the white polystyrene inner changed to a darkish grey foam with a different layout of the accessories. Box alterations seemed to be limited to loading instructions down the left hand side of the box front. Unfortunately, unable to examine rear of the box.

Informed that Gats were available in soft boxes throughout entire production.

Heym pistol.

A post war gat pistol, produced in Germany by the Heym company, an old established company which traded from various different towns at varying times. During the period the pistol was starting production the firm was operating from Muennerstadt.

Estimated production period, from about 1950 until possibly the late 1970's.

Main body of die cast alloy shaped like a Savage pocket automatic pistol, blued steel trigger with black plastic grip panels, steel spring cover partially blued at front end, main frame with fine black crackle paint finish.

Another pistol, unfortunately in relic condition and in pieces had a blued finish with light brown grips, presume this pistol was made earlier than the one illustrated below, also a version has been seen with whitish plastic grips.

Pistol no. 24, left side view showing trademark in circular logo.

Note the trigger stamped from a flat steel plate and the slide with cast in finger grips imitating an automatic pocket pistol.

Pistol no. 24, left side view.

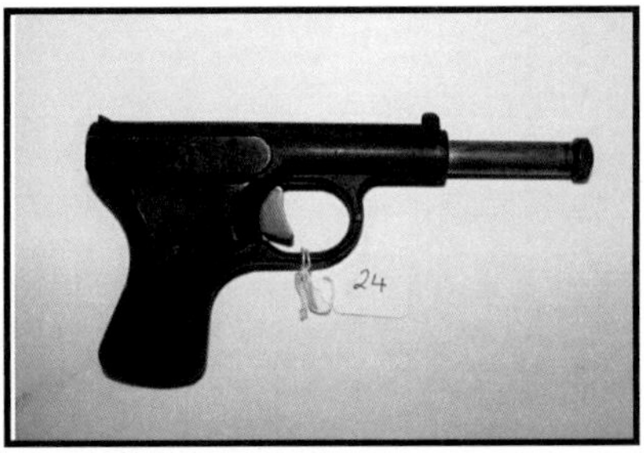

Right side, showing lack of trademark.

In many respects this is one of the best handling and comfortable gats for someone with a smaller hand, however it does appear to be somewhat uncommon. Possibly it was too expensive, but the different types of frame and grip finishes would point to a fairly long production period, maybe it was only made or imported in small quantities, whatever the reason it is a fairly hard one to find, not known if a chrome version was ever produced.

Dimensions.

Overall length. 7 7/8'' 200 mm. Weight. 11 oz 263 grm.

Values.

A bit hard to determine a price but would estimate around £25 to £60.

Auction. None have appeared as separate items in recent auctions.

Notes.

A cutaway drawing of the Heym pistol appears in chapter two of W.H.B Smiths 1957 Gas, Air & Spring Guns of the World and it appears from the text to have been in production for some time, so the estimated date for starting production seems to be reasonable.

Limit.

Yet again a series of tinplate pistols which have almost identical characteristics to the Diana Model 2, the only real distinguishing feature is the trademark which consists of the word Limit in an oval on top of the cylinder. This trademark is very lightly stamped and on rusted examples could easily be missed, also versions seen with inserted plastic grips. Reportedly these pistols were available pre 1939 and were said to be British made, however any pre-war pistols were more probably produced in Germany but this idea has still to be proven

Post war production most probably did take place in Britain as all the pistols seen bear a great resemblance to the Milbro Diana's and especially to the Briton pistol which was also available with inserted plastic grips. Estimated production period around 1939 to possibly 1949, but unlikely any production occurred during the war years, maker is as yet unknown but there is enough similarity between the groups of pistols to wave an uncertain finger somewhat in the direction of Milbro Limited as makers of the post war pistols.

Pistol no. 18, close up of Limit marking with Made in England above.

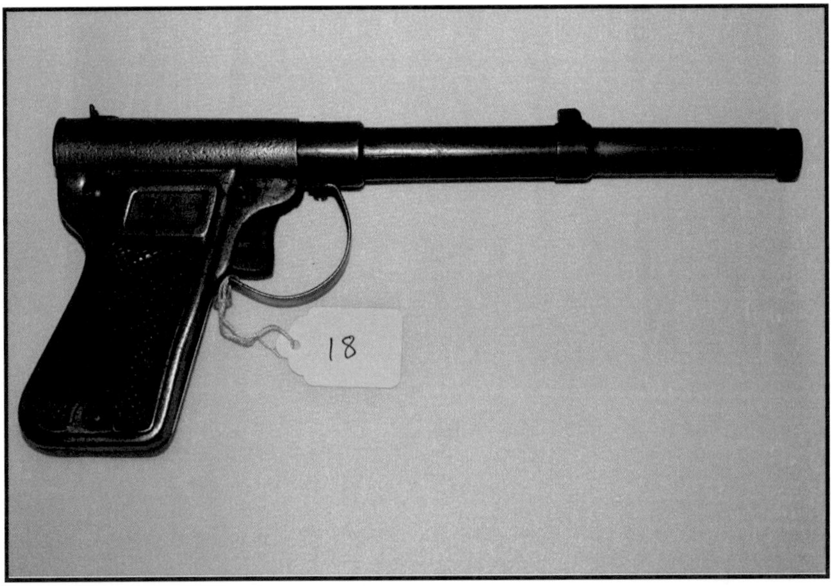

Pistol no. 18, Fairly rough condition but note inserted brown plastic grips.

Pistol no. 18, Compare with the white gripped Briton, note lack of washers.

Dimensions.

Tinplate Limit.

Overall length. 9 7/8'' 251mm. Weight. 11 3/8 oz 322 grm.

Tinplate Limit with inserted plastic grips.

Overall length. 9 7/8'' 251mm. Weight. 11 1/4 oz 328 grm.

Values.

Limit, no pre-war pistols seen so post war prices only, all should be within the £10 to £100 range depending on condition, more if mint and boxed.

Auction. None seen.

Notes.

Scout pistol.

Another of the gat pistols which have yet to be assigned to a particular maker, it has many similarities to the early trigger guard-less Briton pistol which Dennis Hillier cautiously assigned to either Edwin Aston or Frank Clarke, both of Birmingham. The grip plates if inverted appear to be the same outline as the flat base Briton butt and possibly that pistol was a cheaper version of the Scout.

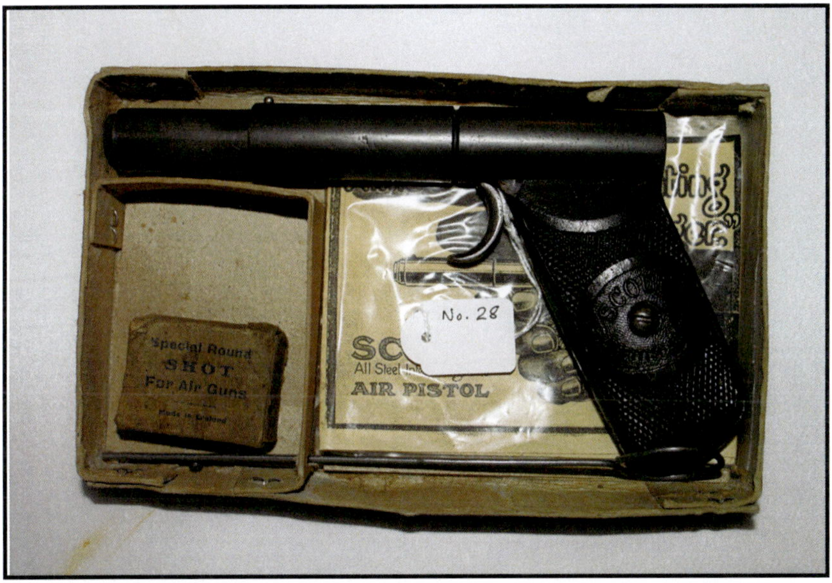

Pistol no. 28, boxed with instructions, wire ramrod and old box for round shot.

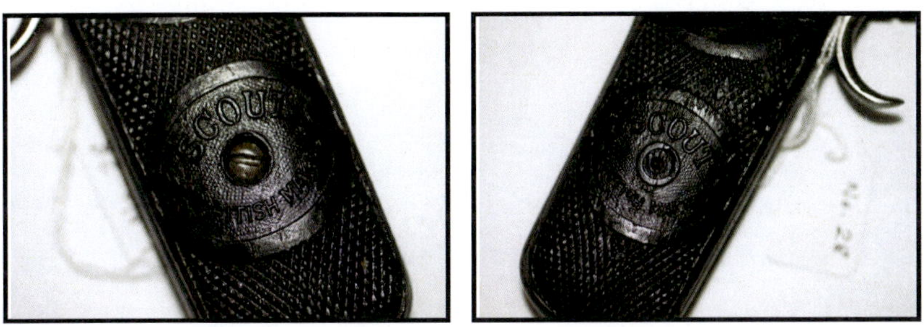

Pistol no.28, left and right grip plate, possibly of compressed horn or plastic.

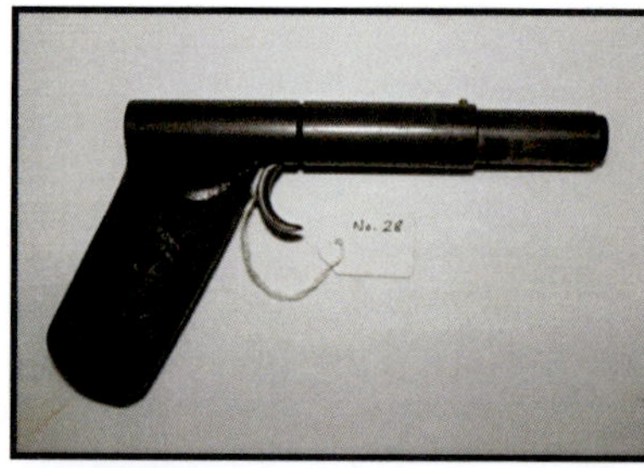

Pistol no.28, near mint condition, left and right side views.

Pistol no.55, relic order, left and right grips showing delamination and cracking.

Pistol no. 28, box lid illustration, paper label on heavy brown pasteboard box.

Front page of Scout instruction leaflet.

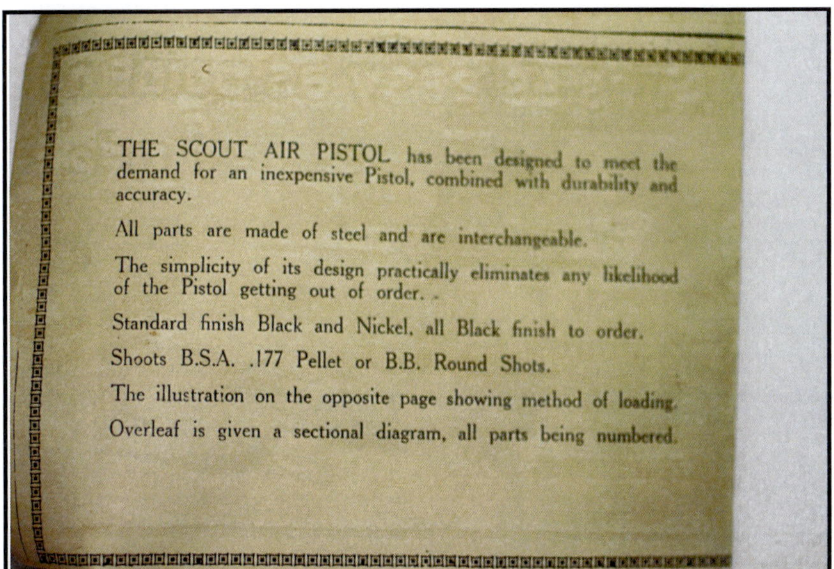
THE SCOUT AIR PISTOL has been designed to meet the demand for an inexpensive Pistol, combined with durability and accuracy.

All parts are made of steel and are interchangeable.

The simplicity of its design practically eliminates any likelihood of the Pistol getting out of order.

Standard finish Black and Nickel, all Black finish to order.

Shoots B.S.A. .177 Pellet or B.B. Round Shots.

The illustration on the opposite page showing method of loading.

Overleaf is given a sectional diagram, all parts being numbered.

Page 2. Note detail about standard finish, most pistols found appear to be black.

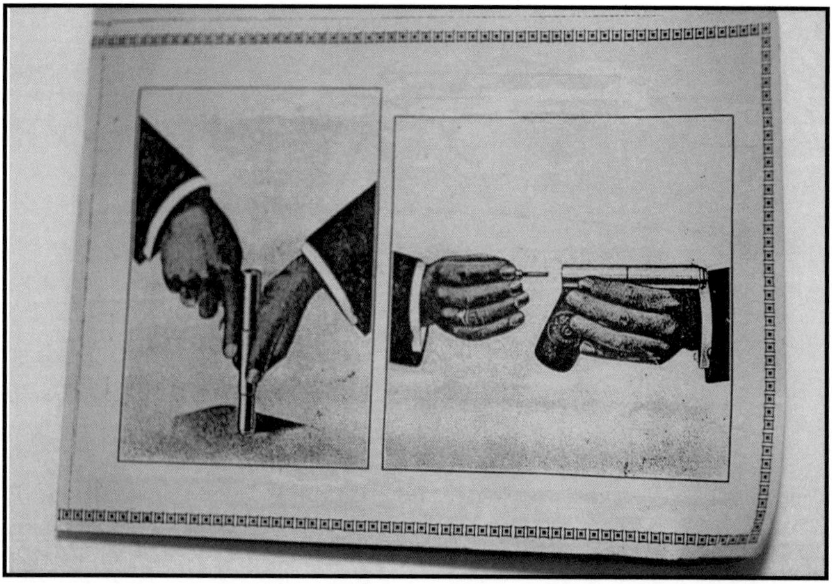

Page 3. Operating instructions.

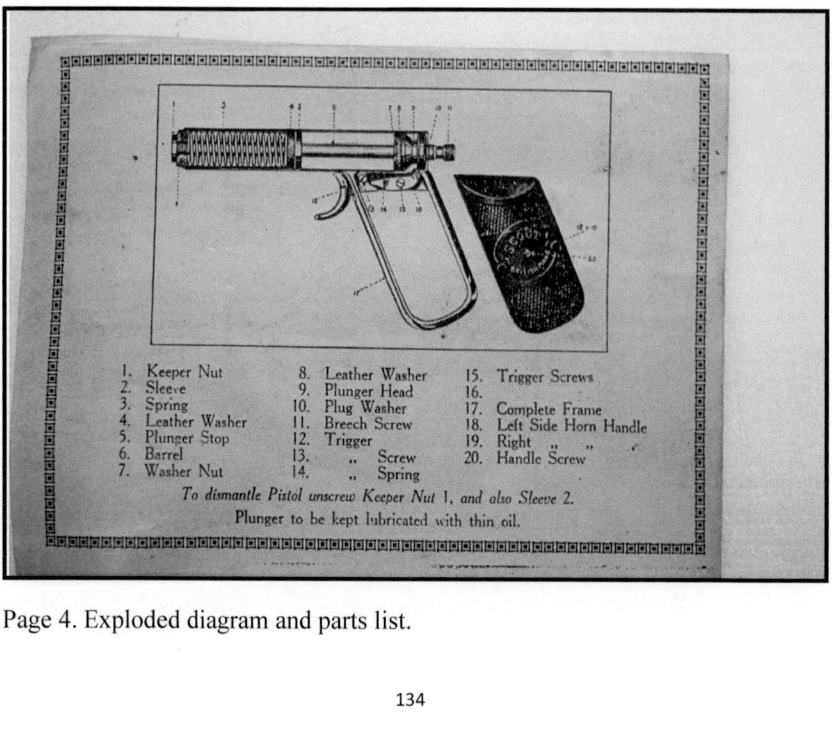

Page 4. Exploded diagram and parts list.

Box for round shot (possibly original).

Dimensions.

Overall length. 7 15/16'' 202mm. Weight. 11 3/4 oz 335grm.

Values.

Brought no. 28 boxed for £250, estimated value unboxed £50 to £200.

Auction. None seen as single lots.

Notes.

According to an article by Doctor Joseph Gilbert in the December 1975 Guns Review, the Scout was seen advertised in 1923 catalogues at 10/-6d (52 1/2p). Interestingly the pistol in that article was all nickel plate which is a different option to those shown in the instruction sheet.

Webley Gnat.

Webley & Scott had been producing revolvers, automatic pistols and shotguns for many years prior to the introduction of air pistols, the first attempt in 1910 was a very advanced design by William Whiting which sadly did not go into production and it was 1924 when the famous and well known Webley air pistols designed by Johnstone and Ferne started production, these pistols in various forms must have had one of the longest production lives ever as they were manufactured for seventy years and only replaced by the Nemesis in 1994. The Nemesis cost £69.95, it's just possible that either the firm needed a cheaper alternative or these gnats were obtained as a stopgap sometime in the 1990's to cover some hiatus in Webley's business or a possible relocation. This gnat was purchased around 2000 at Bisley for £8, brand new in its rather cheap, thin cardboard box, the orange colouring of the box proved to be very transient, in fact it needed to be kept in the dark to prevent rapid and obvious fading. The pistol itself is a one piece hard, brittle plastic casting, on another pistol the foresight had broken. Alloy spring cover with blued steel muzzle nut. Suspect Lov trademark to be East European, possibly made by a CZ subsidiary firm.

Pistol no.25, left side showing stuck on label (34/01) significance unknown.

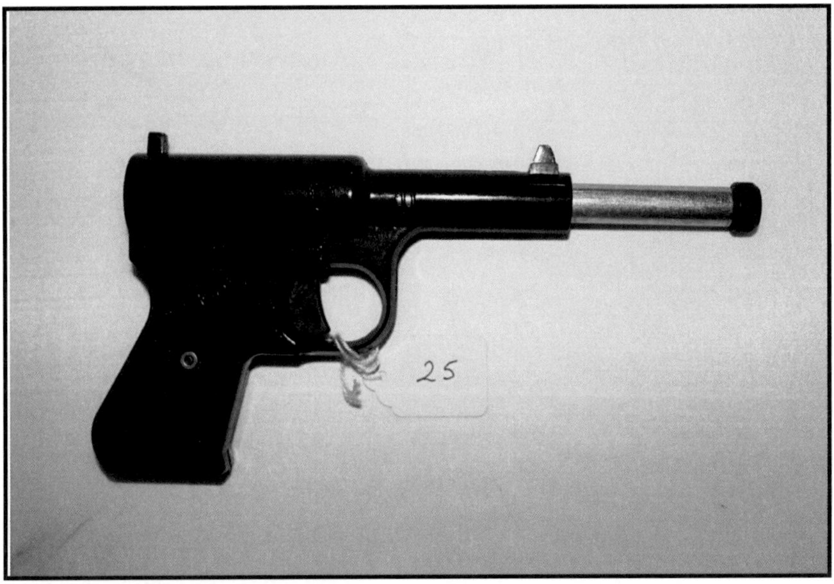

Pistol no. 25, right side view showing Lov trademark in grip.

Pistol no. 25, showing Lov 2 above trigger and oval spring oiling hole.

Pistol no. 25, detail view of trademark, the grip bolt has no apparent function.

Pistol no. 25, detail of easily lost, stuck on grip label.

Detail of faded box, note it was bright orange with bright red GAT of GnAT.

Rear of box showing instructions and what appears to be the CZ trademark.

Side view of box showing distinct use of Webley name.

Dimensions.

Overall length. 8 1/4'' 209mm. Weight. 7 7/8 oz 224 grm.

Values.

Brought in around 2000 for £8, estimate £5 to £35.

Auction. None seen as single lots.

Notes.

A very similar pistol can be seen in the 3rd edition of The Airgun Book by John Walters (1984), named as the HS9A, made by Waffenfabrik Schmidt of West Germany. Apart from the grip medallion and a different shaped foresight the pistol looks identical to the gnat, I suspect that the gnat may have been made much later after production of the HS9A had ceased and manufacture was possibly moved elsewhere to another company.

Unknown gats.

There are many unnamed gat type pistols yet to be discovered, most have little or no recognisable identification markings and are consequently difficult to ascribe to any particular manufacturer.

Boxed unknown pistol.

Advert from 1905 Charles Osbourne & Co. Ltd. trade catalogue.

Pistol no. 71, left side of pistol. For once it compares well with the catalogue.

Pistol no. 71, right side view of cocked pistol.

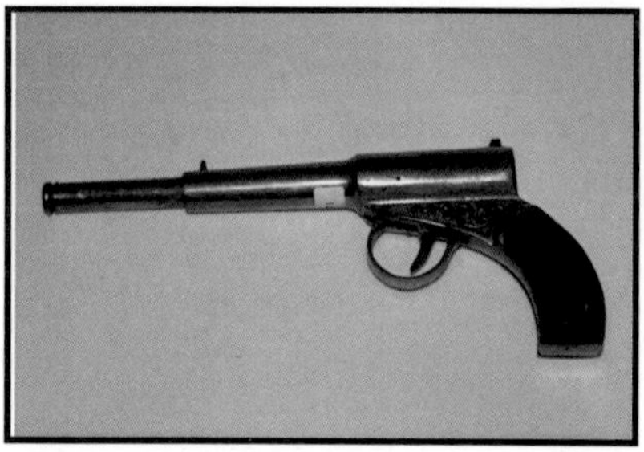

Pistol no. 71, left and right sides of pistol with barrel in fired position.

Advertised trade price in 1905 was 10 shillings (10/-), the same catalogues show black japanned Dolla pistols at 39/- per dozen, allowing that the price of Dolla pistols was around 4/- each retail, the above pistol must have been sold at around 12/- . This would make it a very expensive gat pistol for that period.

Described as no. 1431, Superior nickel plated air pistol, covered spring, vulcanite stock, fitted in black velvet lined case with supply of slugs and darts.

Only marking found on the pistol, is a 2 stamped on the left side of the trigger.

Pistol no. 71, left side foliate panel and tiny oil hole, note 2 stamped on trigger.

Pistol no. 71, in black velvet lined case with original pellet tin (empty).

Dimensions.

Overall length. 8 1/2 " 217mm. Weight. 13 1/4 oz 378 grm.

Values.

Purchased in 2011for £300, boxed and near mint.

Auction. No pistols of this type have appeared at auction.

Other Pistols from Catalogues etc.

Illustration from The Arms and Ammunition Manufacturing Company Limited catalogue of 1904 showing a pistol which also appears in the 1905 Charles Osbourne catalogue without a name but as catalogue number 1429 (see Cast Iron Dolla section). Described as very rare by Alan Harvey. He has only seen and sold one in all the time he has been collecting. Suspect that due to the low price it was cheaply made and looks liable to break across the thin grip section. The burning question is to find out what OPH stands for. It might then be possible to find out the name of the manufacturer.

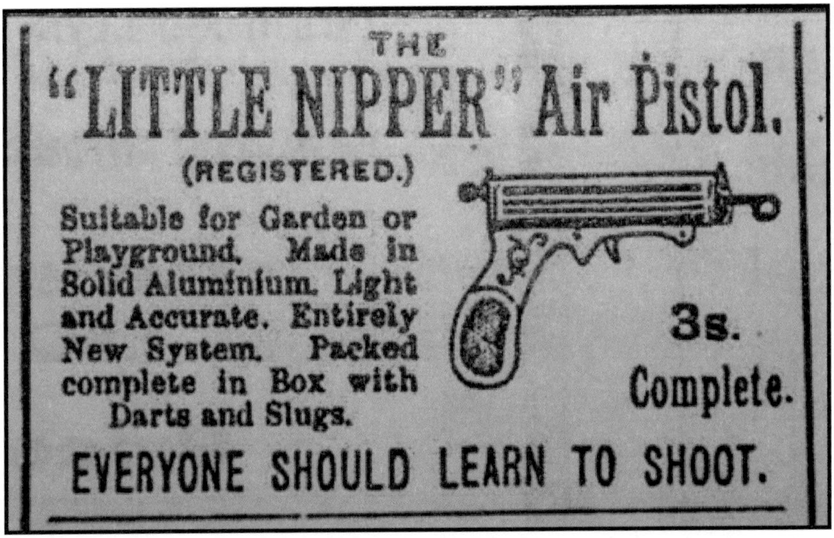

Again from the catalogue of the A. & A. M. Co. Ltd of 1904 was a tiny advert for the Little Nipper. Unfortunately this name is not a lot of use as this firm used Nipper on several of their airguns despite them coming from other makers. However I did manage to get a brief glimpse at a very similar pistol at Bisley Arms Fair some years ago, it has a pull out forward rod to cock the piston with a gat type barrel albeit fixed above the cylinder. Suspect this may be either a French or more likely Belgian pistol.

Again from the A. & A. M. Co. Ltd of 1904 catalogue, a small advert which appeared to show a wooden stocked, nickel plated gat type rifle but in fact turned out to be a one of Mr. Quackenbush's push in airguns.

Notes.

Quasi gats.

Or pistols that are almost but not quite exactly, entirely unlike a Gat!

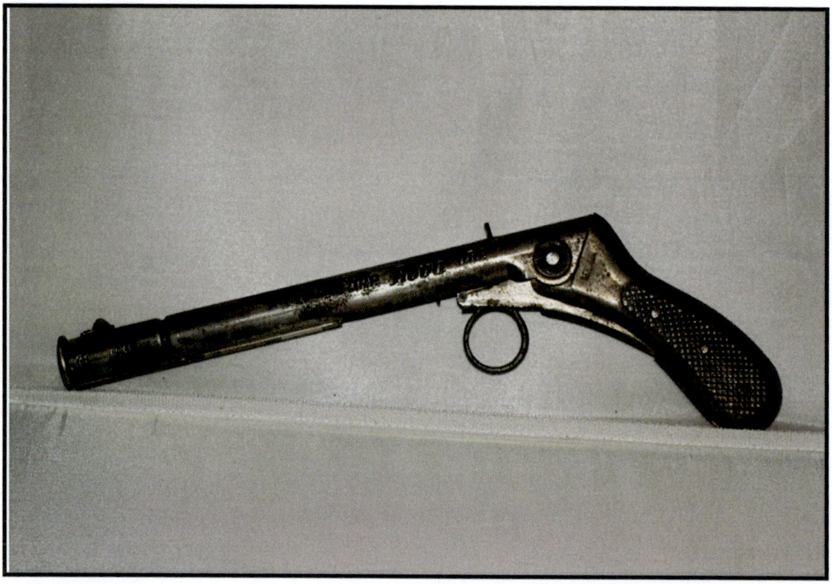

Pistol no. 68, a Nova tinplate cork, dart and pellet pistol, Unknown maker.

O.K. it's not really a gat or anything like one, but as an unlikely survivor of a class of pistol that crosses the line between toy and airgun it deserves to be written about. Operates exactly like the break action popguns of cherished but alas now long past childhood memory, it is made of the cheapest possible riveted heavy tinplate construction, the locking system is by pressed out ribs on the cocking arm which also holds the steel ring trigger. A 2¼ inch bayonet fitting barrel unit with a tapered cork recess and a short brass barrel fits in the end of the barrel shroud. This unit was very easy to lose and then the pistol could easily be mistaken for a standard cork pistol. With the unit removed the pistol could fire ¾ inch corks or more probably the rubber shells which were popular around 1905 to 1914.

DRP marks were for a German design registration system, possibly pre WW1. Was a method of registering the actual design to avoid others copying. After WW1 it became DRGM which stood for Deutsches Reichs Gebrauchsmuster.

Nova Pistol.

Pistol no. 68, cocked with barrel unit removed.

Nova barrel markings left side only.

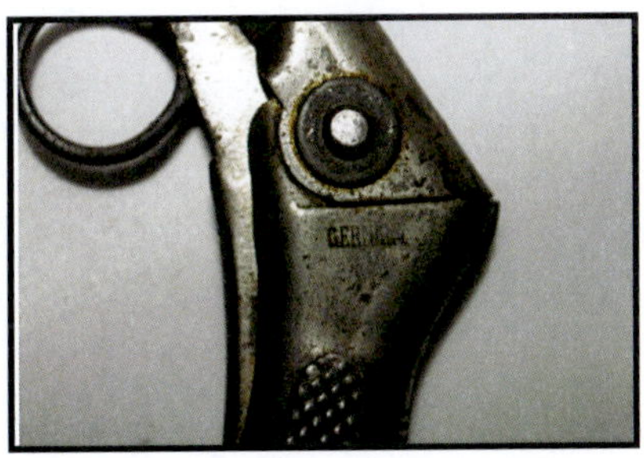

Germany marking behind left breech.

Quesstimate age as just before, or shortly after WW1. Made in Germany.

Would repay further research. The tie up between toys and air-pistol production has not really been looked at as far as I know. A trawl through the relevant toy patents could prove to be a positive goldmine of information about early pistols.

Hubertus Pistol.

Or take a really simple idea and make it so much more awkward. Alternately find a non-existent problem and add lots and lots of complications.

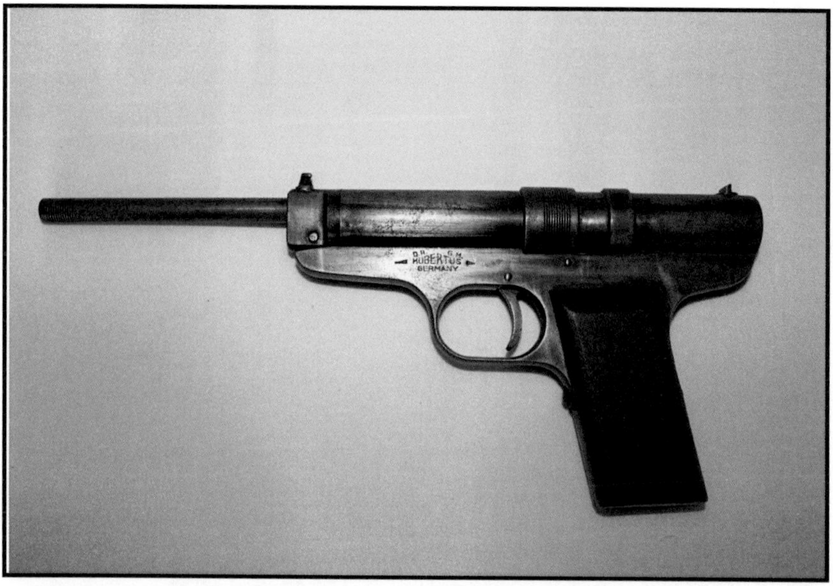

Pistol no. 64, serial no. 2409, in closed fired or firing position.

Barrel pushed in to cock action.

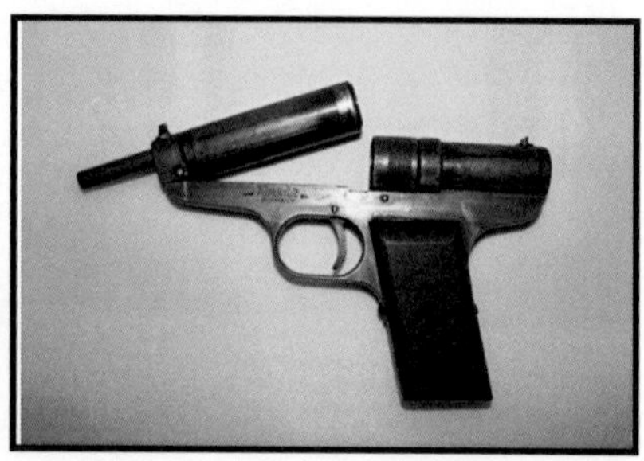

Shroud pushed back and action open.

This pistol has a very complicated interlocking method of operation, to operate first push in the barrel to cock piston, slide back ribbed shroud and tilt barrel unit up. Insert pellet, lower barrel unit and lock with shroud, finally grasp front of barrel and pull out until it stops, at last the pistol is ready to be fired.

Hubertus Pistol.

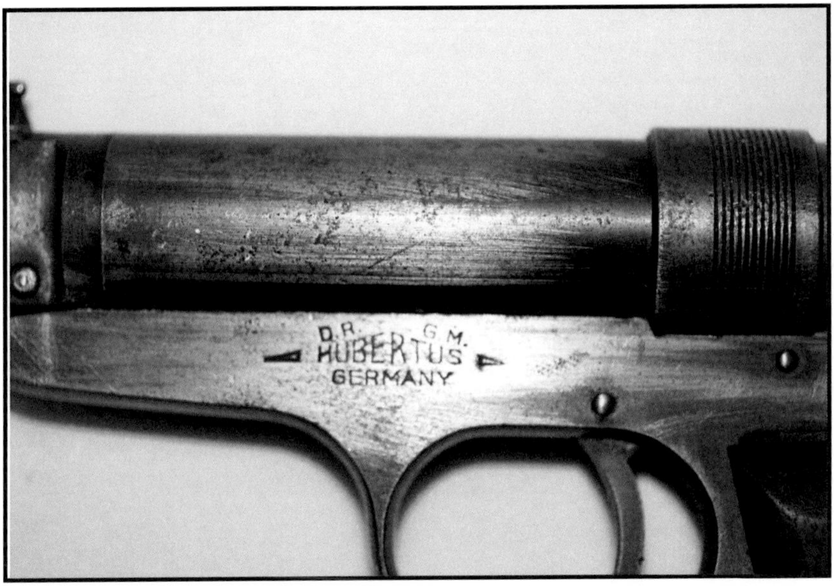

Left side marking, with DRGM Post WW1 Registration markings.

This pistol is made to firearms production standards of manufacture, it must have cost an absolute fortune to produce and is probably as well made as the contemporary Webley pistols, however where the Webley was one of the simplest of pistols to use this is one of the most complex and has a couple of possible problems, the barrel unit can be pushed right out and lost but the most dangerous problem is if the sear lets go, the piston unit can shoot forward and mash fingers against the barrel unit. Produced 1920's to 1930's.

Milbro Cub

Patented by a Frenchman, Rene Boulet of Paris, British patent no. 21954–5 46 was applied for in 1946 and granted in December 1948. However production by Millard Brothers appears to have started around 1947 – 48, the pistol resembles a gat in that the pellet (a lead 2.4mm or no.7 shotgun shot) is fired through a concentric brass barrel by squeezing the rubber bulb in the front of the butt, the shot is retained by a rubber washer until sufficient pressure is built up.

Pistol no. 76, Milbro Cub box lid.

Pistol no. 76, Milbro Cub box showing pistol, sight and charges box.

Pistol no. 76, Left side of pistol showing Milbro Cub on rubber bulb.

Pistol no. 76, Right side of pistol showing thin wire clearing rod.

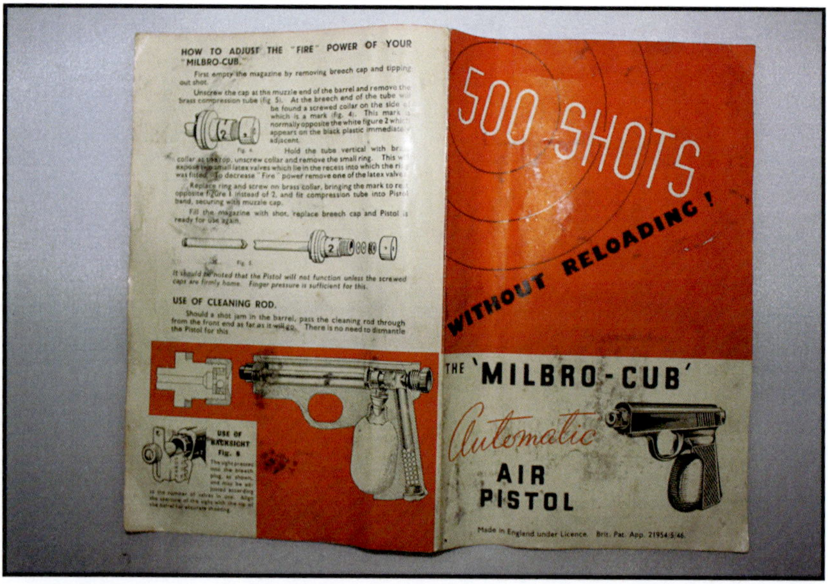

Milbro Cub instruction sheet, rear page has power (?) hop up details.

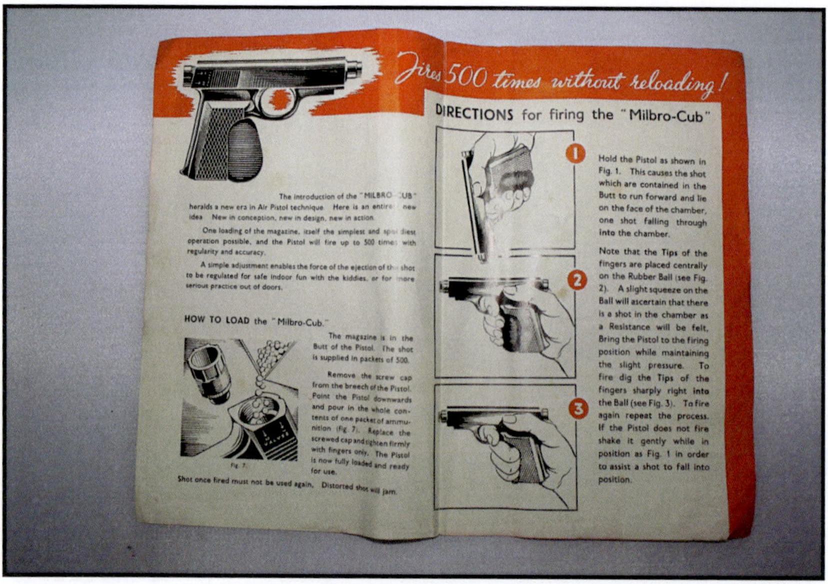

Milbro Cub instruction sheet, middle pages with loading and firing details.

The Milbro Cub was advertised as an 'almost' harmless 500 shot repeater, supplied in a stout cardboard box with a match type box for 2000 charges and a packet of washers, a push in sight, spinning metal disc and cardboard knockdown targets (see Odds and Sods section for details). It was available in polished metal and a purplish blue finish, which appears to be somewhat rarer also sold in France with a longer target barrel. There is a comprehensive write up covering this pistol in Dennis Hillers, 2nd and 3rd editions of Airpistols.

Dimensions. Nova Pistol

Overall length. 11 1/2'' 295mm. Weight. 11 oz 312 grm.

Values.

Based on rarity as only 3 specimens known and value accordingly high, if very lucky and found at a toy fair it might be £10, if not may be up to £200.

Dimensions. Hubertus Pistol

Overall length. 10 1/2'' 248mm. Weight. 1lb 6 3/4 oz 644 grm.

Values.

Condition and correctly operating with all the parts is the main consideration with these pistols, expect to pay £30 for one that needs work up to £175 for minter.

Auction. £100, £30, £70, £60 and £90.

Dimensions. Milbro Cub Pistol

Overall length. 6 1/8'' 155mm. Weight. 10 oz 283 grm.

Values.

Depends a great deal on condition and completeness of the outfit, pistols on their own probably £20 to £60, boxed sets from £100 upwards, each additional item adds significantly to the price due to the rarity, the set shown was £225.

Other Pistols.

Some pistols while not being actual gats do have some of the characteristics. The most obvious similarity is the concentric barrel passing through the piston, the methods of cocking and loading might differ from a gat but examining any of these pistols highlights the different ideas that were developing and shows the logical progression towards a better type of pistol. It's only the cheapness and simplicity of the gat that meant it outlived a lot of the pistols shown below.

Some pistols to research in other books, try to buy or examine in collections.

Maker.	Name.	Cocked by.	Manufactured.
A.B.Vapenfabriken	Excellent	Top lever	ci. 1946 to 59
Accles & Shelvoke Ltd.	Acvoke	Triggerguard	1946 to 1956
Accles & Shelvoke Ltd.	Warrior	Side lever	1930 to 1939
E.Anson	Anson Star	Underlever	1926 to 1930
Fritz Barthelmes.	Record Jumbo	Lift lever	ci. 1980's
Bergmann	Bulldog	Front pull ring	circa 1905
A.A.Brown & Son.	Abas Major	Underlever	ci. mid 40's
Cogswell & Harrison	Certus	Lift/push barrel	1929 to 1930
Daisy.	Targeteer	Top slide	30's to 50's
A.G.Parker	Parker Precision	Crank wound	1921
Produsit Limited.	Big Chief / Thunderbolt Jnr.		1946 to 1949
Sauer & Son.	Tell 2	Triggerguard	1927 to 1936
Westley Richards	Highest Possible		
The concentric barrel version only		Break action	Post 1921
Maker uncertain.	Titan	Rear push rod	ci. 1917 to 1925

See overleaf, I have managed to beg, borrow or (sob!) buy some of the above.

Pistol no. 82, Swedish Excellent pistol serial no. 8279, circa 1957 to 1958.

Pistol no. 82, showing overall very well made and clean design.

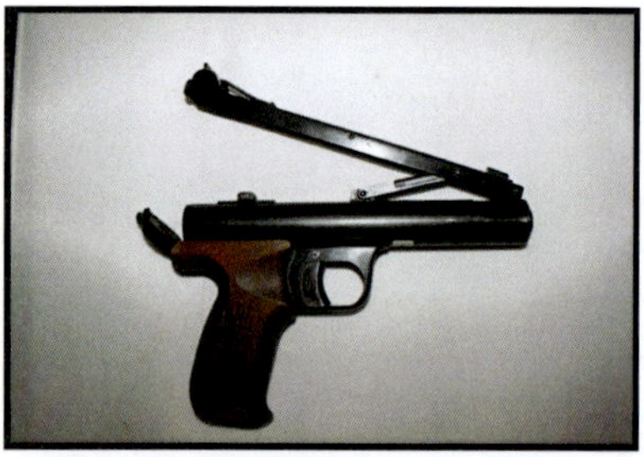

Pistol no. 82, partially cocked. Enlarged view of grip logo.

Pistol no. 82, markings on top of the cocking lever.

One of the few Swedish post war home grown designs, but a really well made and thought out design, although it has some similarities to the Webley barrel cocking pistols, it does address one of the few things that some ham-fisted people criticise about the Webley, which is the tendency to bend the barrel by either applying excessive force to cock or letting it slam shut. The Excellent avoids that problem by using the concentric barrel with a really well sealed end cap. Manufactured by A.B.Vapenfabriken of Sweden, the firm produced just under 9000 pistols of apparently two types between the mid 1940's until production finished in 1959. The serial number of the pistol is 8279 which would seem to place it as a late gun. Nearest British equivalent is probably the side lever Warrior.

Dimensions. Excellent Pistol

Overall length. 8 3/8'' 225mm. Weight. 1lb 12 1/4 oz 800 grm.

Values.

Again condition rules but a good pistol should be around about £400 to £600.

Oak cased Cogswell and Harrison Certus, courtesy of Alan Harvey.

Cogswell and Harrison Trade Label inside lid of oak Certus pistol case.

Left side of Certus, showing various clips, springs and odd bits.

Right side, the workmanship of the fittings leaves a lot to be desired.

Right side, lifting barrel does not cock pistol but opens automatic pellet tap.

Detail of pellet tap operating lever, air nipple and knurled barrel clearing screw.

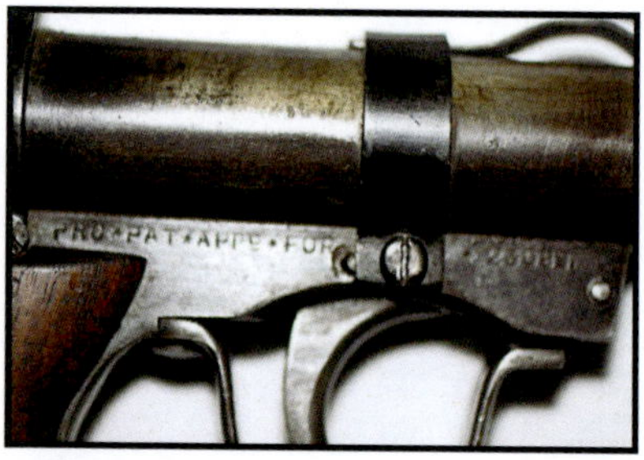

Patent marks on right side.

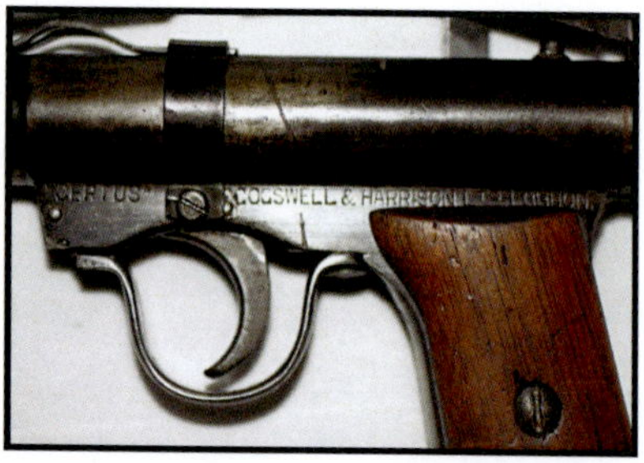

Name and maker on left side

Backstrap of Certus showing two threaded holes for fitting shoulder stock.

Manufactured by Cogswell and Harrison to British patent no. 330105 dated May 9th 1929, which incidentally was not granted. There is a persistent rumour that Webley and Scott had some connection with the Certus and the superficial appearance of the main body of the pistol certainly resembles that of the Webley straight grip Mark I pistol. The quality of the auxiliary fittings however are almost prototypical in appearance and certainly not to the usual standard of either Cogswell and Harrison or Webley, the very short production run of a few months between 1929 and 1930 seem to point to a very unsuccessful pistol. Were these pistols possibly made or finished by the Cogswell apprentices as all the fittings appear to be handmade rather than production items.

Operating the Certus can be likened to rolling about in a cocked bear-trap, the catch under the front of the barrel is released and the barrel raised, this does two things, it operates the automatic loading tap and pulls the cocking arm toward the middle of the pistol under the roller coaster top spring. When the arm reaches the end of the cocking slot it raises slightly under the top spring hump and drops behind the piston lip, pressing down on the very slender barrel, the arm is pushed forward taking the piston with it toward the front of the pistol.

Hopefully this will cock the pistol, but usually if there is the slightest wear in the system the arm slips and the piston flies back, if it cocks a pellet is dropped into the loading tap, the tap is closed and the pistol is ready to fire. An obvious afterthought was the knurled sight retaining screw which had to be removed to clear a stuck pellet. The very weak operating system allied to the numerous crude fittings and obvious hand finishing is probably the reason this pistol was such a failure compared to the robust and simple Webley. Serial number for this pistol is no. 215. Best feature of the whole outfit is the splendid oak case.

Dimensions. Certus Pistol

Overall length. 8 15/16'' 225mm. Weight. 2 lb 1 oz 938 grm.

Values.

Represents one of the Holy Grails of collectable British airguns and prices reflect that. These are significantly rare pistols and are unlikely to be available at less than £1000 +, add a significant premium for an original cardboard box and around £400 to £600 for the oak pistol case.

Pistol no. 81, Parker Precision crank wound pistol circa 1920 -1921.

Pistol no. 81, Left side showing heavy side plate and securing bolts.

Serial no. 214 on end cap.

Gate open showing wire pellet pusher.

Pistol no. 81, The Parker Precision pistol was patented on May 11th 1920, by A.T.C. Hale and E.E. Harris, however the patent was not actually granted. This is a large, heavy, well-engineered pistol with blued finish and apparently case hardened action side-plates, no markings except for serial no. 214 under loading gate at rear of pistol. Operated by rotating crank just over three turns in a clockwise direction until cocked, the crank automatically disengages and pellet can be loaded by rotating gate at rear of pistol sideways and using attached heavy gauge pusher wire to insert pellet. Short lived production around 1921.

Dimensions. Parker Precision Pistol

Overall length. 10 1/2" 267mm. Weight. 2 lb 13 1/4 oz 1282 grm.

Values.

While not quite as rare as the Certus pistol but with nearly as short a production run the Parker is also a valuable collector's item. Prices depend on condition and whether the pistol is original as there are rumours that some were assembled much later from old stock parts. Have been seen for sale at £360 and £500. Add a very significant premium for the dedicated round topped box which apparently takes the pistol stored in a vertical position.

Auction.

Recent auction estimate for a forthcoming sale was £500 to £700 for an untested pistol in reasonable condition albeit with a slightly faded finish.

Pistol no. 76, Record Jumbo outer cardboard wrapper

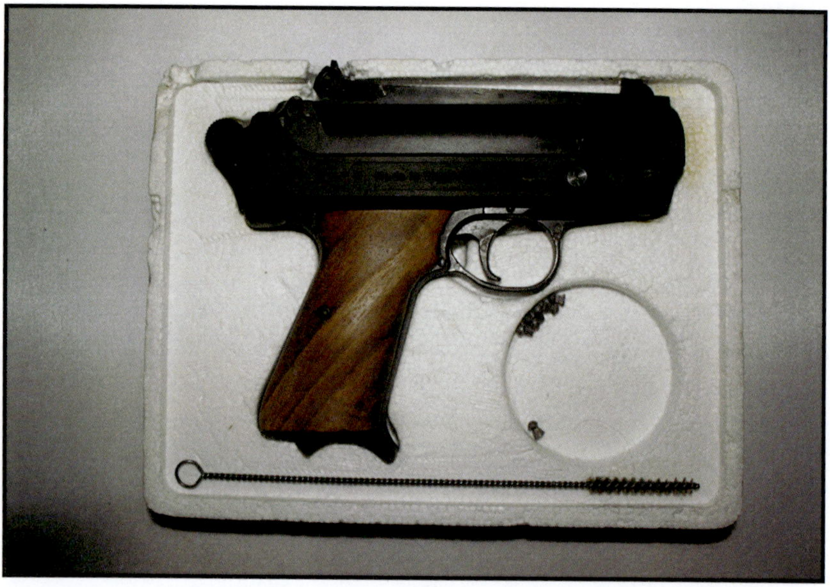

Pistol no. 76, Record Jumbo, inner polystyrene box with clearing rod.

Pistol no. 76, Left side.

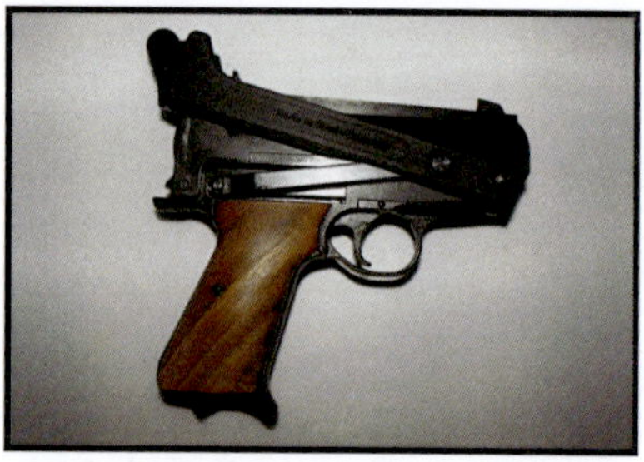

Pistol no. 76, partially cocked.

Jumbo's were available with both fixed and adjustable sights. Also fitted with flat chequered, shaped plain walnut (as above) or extremely expensive German style oak leaf carved walnut grips.

Notes.

Of the other pistols in the listing, the Warrior can be found in the Bourne and Son advert in the Harrington Gat section, the Bergmann Bulldog may be the Little Nipper shown in the A. & A. M. Co. advert in the Unknown section.

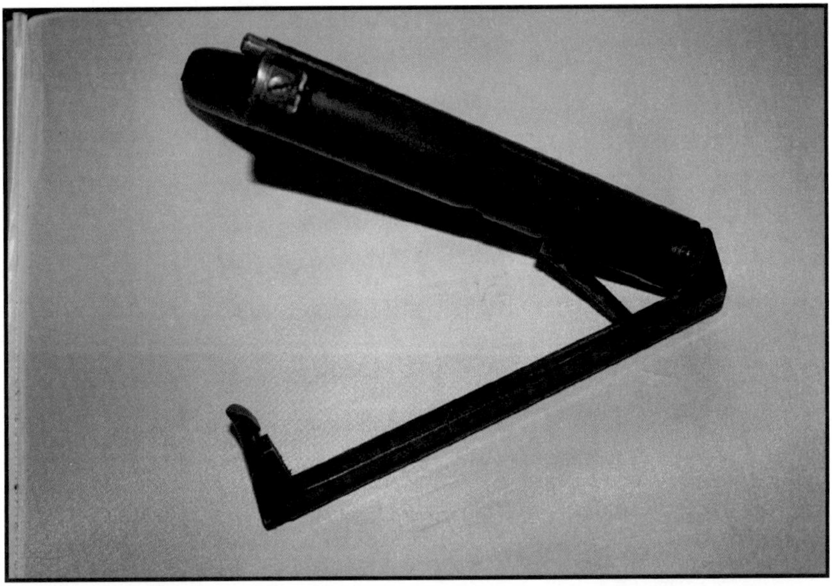

Warrior in cocked position, earlier pistols have angled front to cocking lever.

Warrior. Made to Frank Clarks British patent 351268. Circa 1930 to 1939.

Dimensions. Warrior

Overall length. 8'' 204mm. Weight. 1 lb 13 3/4 oz 841 grm.

Values.

Depends on condition, but prices are increasing, rough ones can be less than £25, rising to over £400 for a minter, add premium for a box. (very rare in .22).

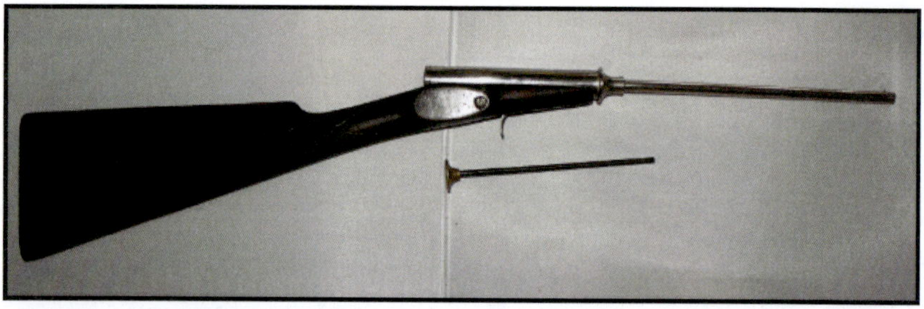

Bussey's airgun. British patent 526 of 1876. Courtesy of Alan Harvey.

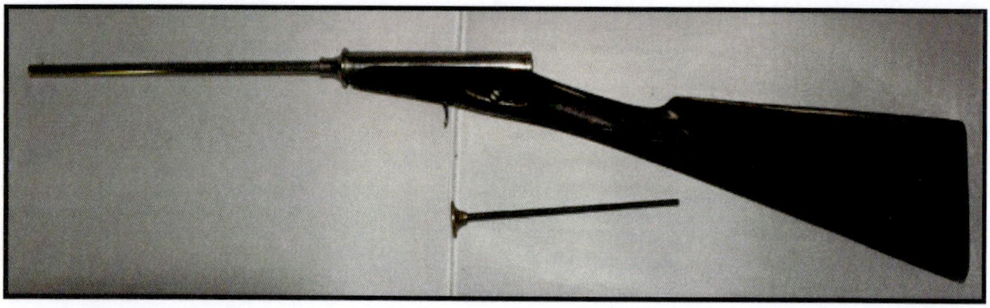

Later versions have trigger-guards and different frame beneath cylinder.

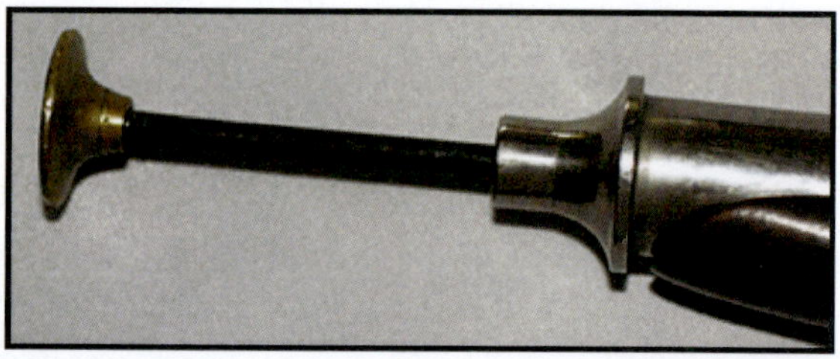

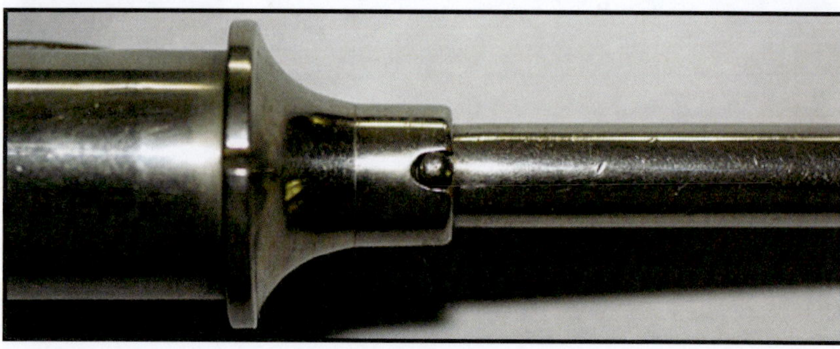

End cap details, cocking rod in use and details of peg and taper barrel joint.

Made by George Gibson Bussey of Museum Works, Rye Lane, Peckham, Surrey. The firm existed by that name from around 1870 to 1883 when it changed to G. Bussey & Co. Ltd. until 1889, the firm continued until 1914 when it possibly converted to munitions work not reappearing after WW1.

Dimensions. Bussey's airgun

Overall length. 27 5/8'' 700mm. Weight. 1 lb 8 3/4 oz 701 grm.

Values.

Unknown, even Beeman's Blue Book says it is extremely rare, so rare that it has no pricing information shown at all, not even an estimate.

Auction.

Well, none have been seen in auction for years and years, this gun could either not sell because no-one recognises how rare it is, or more likely as these guns are avidly sought after by really serious collectors there may well be a bidding war of epic dimensions. Suspect price is going to go well into four figures.

Notes.

Yes indeed the Bussey did make over the £1000, £800 plus premium to be exact and was probably a genuine bargain even at that price.

Odds n Sods.

Ali Baba shooting arcade for Nova type pistols. Figures suspended on elastic.

Arcade ready for use. Ali Baba in the middle with four thieves in oil barrels.

Details of released figures, all about three inches high.

French made for use with cork pistols, circa 1910. Courtesy of Alan Harvey.

Milbro Cub Accessories.

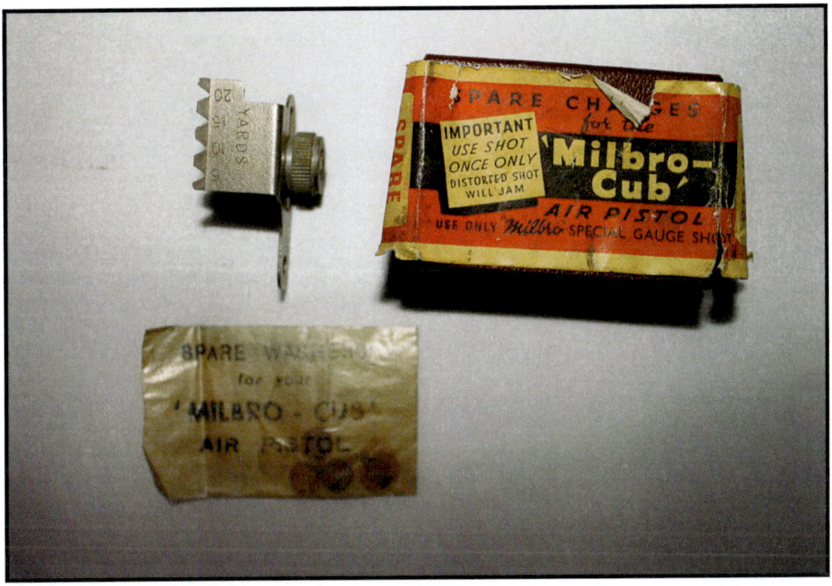

Milbro Cub accessories, match type charges box, push in sight and washer pack.

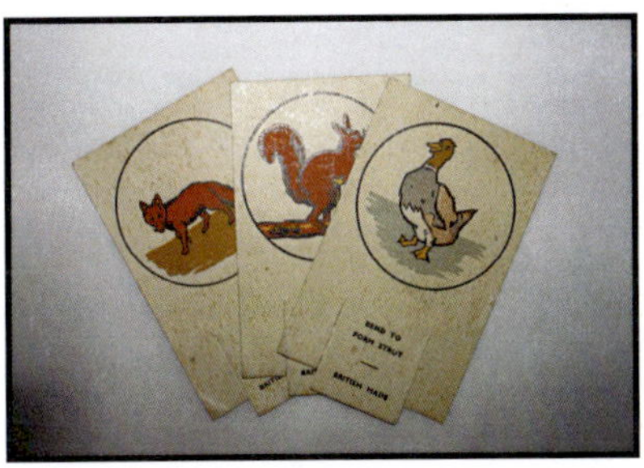

Milbro Cub folding card targets.

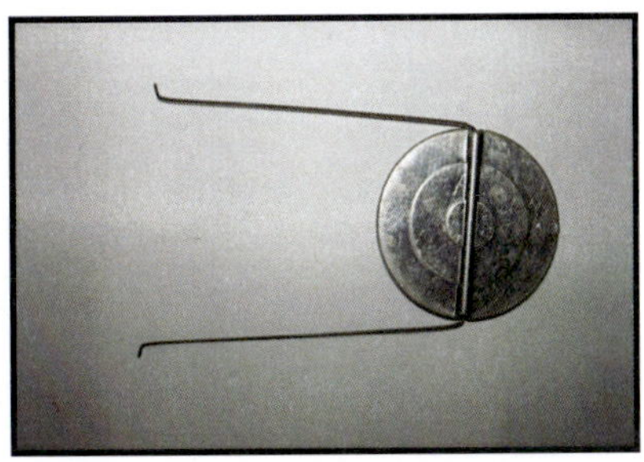

Milbro Cub spinning metal target.

The Milbro Cub was supplied in a card box with a match type box with four packets of charges each containing five hundred 2.4mm shot, a packet of spare shot retaining washers, instruction sheet, push in sight optimistically graduated from five to twenty yards, folding card knock down animal targets and a spinning alloy metal target on spring wire legs. Discussions between collectors appear to agree that there should be five animal card targets in the set.

Little Bits.

My all time favourite pellet box. Cat slugs, favourite fodder for gats.

Rather battered Webley target holder from a Webley Falcon air rifle kit and an original packet of 25 Webley no. 4 targets, unfortunately most have been used.

Complete packet of 25 Diana/Milbro card targets. Circa 1970's, price then 30p.

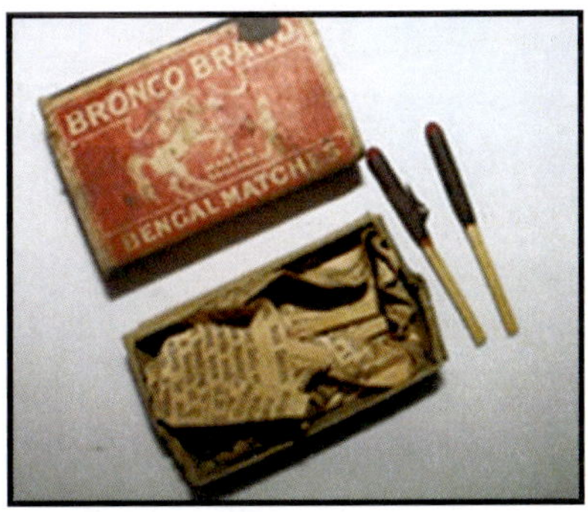

Box top really explains everything.

Red Bengal matches (also in green).

Bengal matches were a childhood favourite and were much used in Gats to provide flare illumination during night-time battles in the sandpit, available either in red or green, the boxes and the inner newspaper wrapping were coloured to indicate the contents, which if I remember correctly were remarkably few per box and seemed to decrease in number as time passed. The green always seemed to burn better and longer than the reds. I think the price used to be three pence (1 1/4p) a box.

Discofelts were introduced around the 1980's as shooters started to become more concerned with accuracy and airguns were moving out of the plinking era into serious target and hunting use. Designed to be shot through rifled barrels to remove fouling and oil residue, some people also used them for short range indoor practice.

WARNING. Most of the projectiles shown below have a hard metal content and there is a significant danger of ricochets, always use eye protection and make sure there is a safe backstop, pellets are cheap, eyes are priceless.

Sussex Armoury (1968 to 1983) made these composite pellets in the late 1970's to early 1980's as an attempt to get higher velocities from a .22 with a solid projectile, unfortunately the sabot made it difficult to load, although a pen like pusher unit was provided which held the projectile together until inserted into an airgun. However it was found that they were unsuitable for airguns with tap or sliding breeches and combined with the high cost, quickly fell out of use.

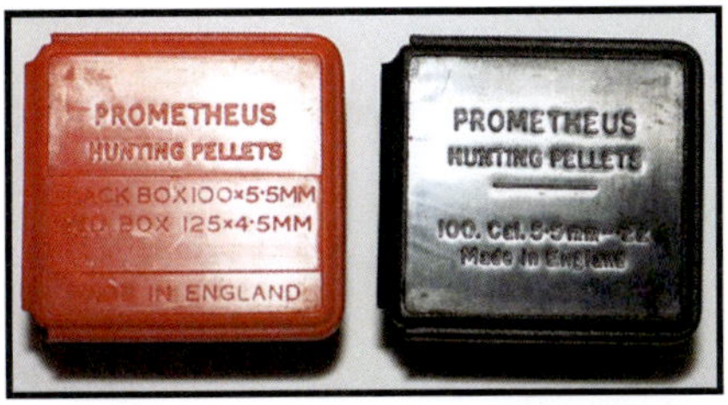

Prometheus .177 and .22 packaging.

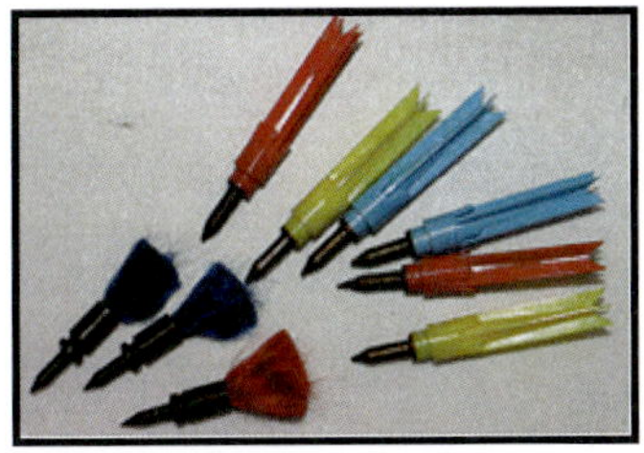

Darts old and short lived new.

Prometheus .177, .22 and Sabo's.

Various packs of steel BB's.

Notes.

Prometheus composite pellets were first produced in 1979 following an earlier small scale experimental production run of the now extremely rare Mirrel pellet produced to British patent no. 2023779, issued to H. Earl. Early batches were found to be inaccurate but by 1981 following modification had been much improved and became more accurate. Only really suited to powerful rifles the pellets skirts were black for .177 and clear for .22 but it is noticeable that the .22 skirts discoloured and deteriorated with time.

Darts were produced for many years prior to 1900, versions for gallery airguns had long tails with a single coloured thread designed as a positioning aid. Later versions were shorter in body and tail and were produced for many years but without their packaging it is difficult to assign them to a particular maker. Designed for use in smoothbore barrels only there was sufficient windage for the steel dart body to rattle around if fired through a rifled bore with the obvious chance of damage, the later plastic bodied darts could be fired through rifling but by the time they were introduced in the late 1970's air-gunning and legislation had moved on and darts were starting to become redundant.

Helpful Books, Catalogues and Magazines.

Airgun World, 2011. Buyers Guide 11. Lists current Air and Gas guns, accessories and has sections giving advice on how to choose, where to buy and much more.

Armoury Publications/H.M.S.O. 1855 to 1930. Patents for Inventions, Class 119 Small Arms. Reprint of a monumental work, expensive but a set of books that I would not be without, contains abridged details of every British small arms patent mostly with an illustration of the major details, an invaluable research resource.

Robert D. Beeman and John B. Allen, 2010. Blue Book of Airguns 8th edition. Has to be the air gunners bible, a massive book of over 500 pages stuffed full of information and illustrations, gives details of Quackenbush's involvement with the various other American makers. The book also contains an excellent method of condition grading and although the prices shown reflect American collecting preferences the book does contain information on lots of rare and scarce items.

David Byron, 1979. Gunmarks. This book contains hundreds of drawings of gun markings, although it has a somewhat confusing layout and mostly covers firearms it does identify lots of previously unrecognised markings and includes German ordnance codes in the names and codes section.

Gordon Bruce, 2001. Webley Air Pistols. An in depth study of the history and development of Webley air pistols, does contain an early chapter covering other makes and patents, a must for the Webley collector.

Dennis E. Hiller, various dates and various editions of the Collectors Guide to Air Pistols (3 editions) and the Collectors Guide to Air Rifles (4 editions); these are the books that really started raising the collectors interest in airguns. I bitterly regret having sold the first editions in a moment of penury but we all do silly things sometimes, recommended well detailed books, good coverage of pellet packaging in later editions.

Joseph J. Schroeder (editor). Rare selections from Old Gun Catalogues, 1880 to 1920, not a lot of airguns but a fascinating array of firearms and shows the progression of the various types of advertising and illustration across the ages.

W. H. B. Smith, 1957. Gas, Air and Spring Guns of the World. One of the classic works on air guns, somewhat difficult layout and some of the information has been superseded by later research, but still a worthwhile book to have on the shelf.

John Walter, 1984. The Airgun Book, 3rd edition. Some early airguns covered but mainly 1970's to 80's production, good sections on chronographs, ammunition and testing data.

L. Westley, Airguns and Airpistols, revised 1961. A well written early book with a few dating faults possibly caused by using text from the 1955 edition, but has excellent advice on what not to do with air canes indoors (or outdoors) and although the law has changed somewhat, good chapters on the early power testing used to set lawful power levels, garden ranges, collecting and maintenance.

Catalogues.

I managed to obtain a large amount of useful catalogues directly from America via Cornell Publications over the Internet. (www.cornellpubs.com). The firms contact is the ever helpful Abby (abby@cornellpubs.com) who is a delight to deal with, the company reproduces literally thousands of gun related catalogues and leaflets, there is also an online newsletter which is well worth viewing especially the Rants and Raves section which proves Darwin could be wrong.

Catalogues with airgun data obtained from Cornell Publications in date order.

James Brown and Son, Pittsburgh, U.S.A. 1876

C. G. Bonehill, Birmingham, England . 1888

Issac Hollis and Sons, London and Birmingham, England. 1893

Frank Dyke and Company, London Wholesalers, England. ci. 1900

Arms and Ammunition Manufacturing Co. Ltd. London, England. 1904

Charles Osbourne and Company Limited, Birmingham, England. 1905

W.W.Greener, London and Birmingham, England. 1906

Westly Richards and Company Limited. ci. 1908 – 1910

G. and M. Clyde, Glasgow, Scotland. 1910

W. J. Jeffery and Company Limited, London, England. ci. 1910 – 1911

Adolf Frank Export Gesellschaft, Hamburg, Germany. 1911

Joseph Bourne and Sons, Birmingham, England. 1912

Midland Gun Company, Birmingham, England. 1914

L. Le Personne and Company, London, England. 1925

Shoverling, Daly and Gales, New York, U.S.A. 1925

L. Oppleman Importer, Lynchburg and New York, U.S.A. 1930

Joseph Bourne and Son, Birmingham, England. 1933

Georg Frank (WUM), Hamburg, Germany. 1937

Stoeger Arms Company, U.S.A . Airguns of the World. 1939

Other Catalogues and Leaflets.

While there may not be a huge amount of airgun coverage in any of the catalogues shown they are great sources of information on all sorts of things.

Manton and Company, Calcutta and Delhi, India. 1926 - 1927

W. Darlow, Wholesaler, Bedford, England. 1928

Webley and Scott Limited, Birmingham, England. 1914

J.L.S. Arms, Wednesbury, West Midlands, England 1981

Battle Orders, East Sussex, England. Various editions

Phoenix Arms Company Limited, East Sussex, England. Various editions

Parker Hale, Birmingham, England. Various editions

Henry Krank, Pudsey, West Yorkshire, England. Various editions

World Wide Arms Limited, Birmingham, England. Various editions

Magazines.

Guns Review. 1960's to the late 90's. Alas a sadly now defunct publication, which closed following the passing of the completely useless Handgun Ban, a brilliant monthly magazine covering all aspects of shooting, history, gunmakers, cartridges and military weapons had especially good coverage of airguns from the 1970's onward following the pioneering Airgun Scene articles from the greatly underrated Dennis Commins, a real gentleman and very generous at sharing information. Also, numerous in depth articles of exhaustive research by Doctor Joseph S. E. Gilbert. Lots of airgun articles from such contributors as Geoffrey Allen, M. H. Newcomer, Chris Risebrook and many others. Wish this magazine was still going as I subscribed to it for over thirty years and when it disappeared, it left a huge void in historic research which no general magazine has ever really got close to replicating.

Airgun World and Airgunner. Airgun World started in 1977, a dedicated magazine for airguns with a large amount of articles directed towards the vintage and collector airguns, it was joined by the Airgunner, both magazines are now being produced by the same publisher. The magazines have enjoyed the services of many great contributors between them over the years and although the coverage and contents vary between the two magazines both provide lots of information about older airguns.

Gun Mart. Large monthly magazine with extensive coverage of shooting, re-enactment and auctions, includes a large dedicated section for airguns, has a huge amount of items for sale in each issue with extensive advertising and also includes details of forthcoming arms fairs.

Shooting Times. Country sporting magazine dedicated to all aspects of field sports, has occasional excellent airgun articles plus much other interesting coverage of a wide range of subjects.

Most other advertising magazines now refuse to carry adverts for anything to do with shooting but occasionally airguns can be found in local free and localized area weekly advertising papers, it may prove to be difficult to find any major treasures but you never know what can turn up.

Chronograph test results.

Method:
Velocity Calculations.

Pistols were tested over a series of 10 shots using Eley Wasp .177 (7.16 grain) and .22 Milbro Caledonian (13 grain) diabalo roundhead waisted pellets, the results when averaged gave the average velocity.

Foot / Pounds

This was calculated using the Crony information supplied with the chronograph and used the following formula:

Average Velocity x Ave. Velocity x weight of pellet in grains
Divided by 450240 = Foot / Pounds.

Velocities in fps over ten shots.

Pistol No.	**Type.**	**1**	**2**	**3**	**4**	**5**	**6**	**7**
Check	Webley Junior	278.6	283.5	280.2	286.3	280.8	267	284.9
1	Gat Type 1	216.7	214.9	223.9	222	225.3	222.3	225.9
4	Diana M2 Wood	211.1	210.1	223.3	235.5	241.6	231.4	227.1
13	Britannia	153.6	175.6	173	171.1	182.5	190	200.6
14	Cast Iron Dolla	149.2	128.7	159.9	142.3	150.2	139.7	123.7
23	Diana G2/5	271.7	276.5	274.6	279.1	275.9	276.5	287.8
24	Heym	135.3	146.1	147.5	151.5	153.9	154.1	164.4
25	Webley Gnat (Lov2)	168.7	168.3	174	173	171.9	172.9	167.8
28	Scout	191.8	192.1	193.7	197.5	198.4	189.9	197.3
29	Anson Firefly	226.9	217.1	220.3	224	224.5	220.7	190.6
36	Champion	287.6	282.3	289.8	294	279.1	280.8	294.9
37	0.22 Hy-Score	204.1	208	201.9	204.1	205.2	200.4	205.2
51	Dolla Mark II	183.8	195.2	196.1	202.2	210.5	208	216
57	Barnett	246.4	266.4	260.1	257	267.5	253.4	250.6
58	Gat Rifle	436.9	395.4	392.5	464.8	383.1	377.8	452
59	Gat Type 2	130.8	129.3	132.2	129.9	131.1	128.4	129.6
68	Nuvo	87.4	88.97	93.21	89.99	81.34	89.35	91.89
71	Unknown Pistol	133.1	128.9	133.9	138.6	139.4	137.9	128.5
72	Diana Model 1	243.3	245.7	246.2	246.3	242.3	247.9	245.9
79	MGR	125.8	91.35	72.26	92.6	149.1	167.1	93.32
81	Parker Crank Wind	415.6	411.1	395.6	416.5	426.8	412.3	408.1
82	Swedish Excellent	240.3	246.7	254.8	254.7	222.9	256.9	194.7
84	Original modern grip	258.1	266.5	266.6	269.4	288.1	272.3	279
85	Milbro Nickel	192.9	212.5	191.9	210.2	188	210.6	190.1

Using that most desirable of all schoolboy pistols, a mint, almost unused Webley post-war Junior as a benchmark, various gats were tested with the most surprising results. The chronograph testing showed that some of these pistols have substantial power fluctuations and are much less powerful than expected.

The main surprise was the Parker Crank wind pistol, it appeared to be very powerful given the effort required to cock it and the large muzzle blast when it was fired, however when the calculations were completed it was disappointing to find that the power was less than half of the British six foot/pound power limit.

Some pistols were obviously suffering from their age and misuse, but even the weakest was still capable of flattening the head of a pellet.

Pistol No.	**Type.**	**8**	**9**	**10**	**Ave. Vel.**	**Pellet Weight**	**ft/lbs.**
Check	Webley Junior	282.8	278.3	280.5	**279.53**	7.16	**1.24**
1	Gat Type 1	229.1	221.9	228	**222.35**	7.16	**0.79**
4	Diana M2 Wood	227.3	234.7	230.3	**220.7**	7.16	**0.77**
13	Britannia	179.7	193.1	193.5	**181.27**	7.16	**0.52**
14	Cast Iron Dolla	162.3	130.7	122.3	**140.9**	7.16	**0.32**
23	Diana G2/5	277.8	282.8	289.8	**279.25**	7.16	**1.24**
24	Heym	156.9	157.7	152.5	**151.99**	7.16	**0.37**
25	Webley Gnat (Lov2)	177	179	173	**172.56**	7.16	**0.47**
28	Scout	190.4	196.9	195.6	**194.36**	7.16	**0.60**
29	Anson Firefly	217.4	206.4	223.9	**217.18**	7.16	**0.75**
36	Champion	276.6	281.1	280.6	**284.68**	7.16	**1.29**
37	0.22 Hy-Score	207.1	216.7	210.9	**201.9**	13	**1.23**
51	Dolla Mark II	219	197.6	190.6	**201.69**	7.16	**0.65**
57	Barnett	255	251.7	254.5	**256.26**	7.16	**1.04**
58	Gat Rifle	455.1	415.7	432	**420.53**	7.16	**2.81**
59	Gat Type 2	128.4	128.2	127.5	**130.19**	7.16	**0.27**
68	Nuvo	72.53	90.86	88.88	**87.44**	7.16	**0.12**
71	Unknown Pistol	124.1	127.3	125	**131.67**	7.16	**0.28**
72	Diana Model 1	238.7	238	233	**242.73**	7.16	**0.94**
79	MGR	124.3	196.7	190.6	**130.31**	7.16	**0.27**
81	Parker Crank Wind	435.1	421.4	417.8	**416.03**	7.16	**2.75**
82	Swedish Excellent	207.3	204.9	236.8	**232**	7.16	**0.86**
84	Original modern grip	267.7	275.5	266.6	**270.98**	7.16	**1.17**
85	Milbro Nickel	203.3	203.5	209	**201.2**	7.16	**0.64**

Maintenance and Repair.

Gat type pistols, due to their inexpensive and very basic construction often receive little or no maintenance but conversely the basic construction also means there is little to go wrong with them. Faults are usually confined to failure to cock, trigger spring breakage or misplacement, loss of the pellet pusher pin and loss or disintegration of the sealing washers.

Although gats can be stripped with various household tools it is always better NOT to use pliers or a vice directly to hold muzzle nuts and barrels as these can leave prominent tool marks on the metal of the pistol.

Details of a few simple to make tools are given below. These can be modified to suit various gats, a small strip of leather or wooden clothes peg is useful to pad plier jaws when holding a barrel and with the addition of a few good quality screwdrivers anyone should be able to tackle any of the listed repairs.

Basic Tools.

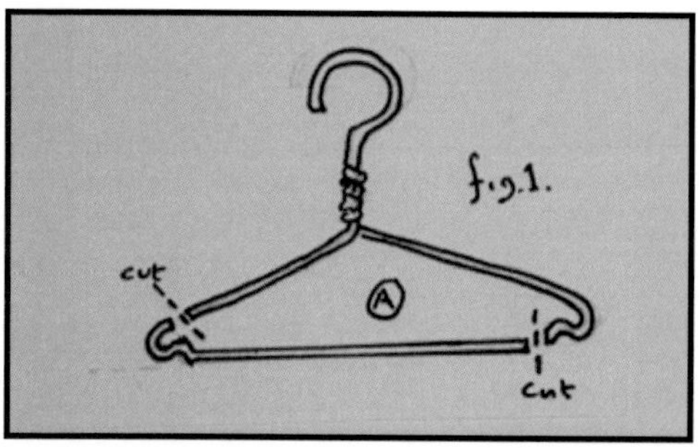

Figure 1. Clearing rod from wire coathanger, Figure 2. Wooden vice block.

Figure one, the diagram shows a wire coat hanger, cuts are made as shown and the curved end is straightened and then bent in the opposite direction to form a loop handle, file the other end of the rod flat to save scratching the barrel.

Figure two, is a set of vice blocks made from two sections of a semi hard wood, approximately two by one inch and three or four inches long, these are clamped together in a vice and a hole slightly smaller than the diameter of the muzzle nut bored through the middle join of the two blocks, in use the muzzle nut is placed between the blocks and the blocks clamped in the vice, holding the nut securely and without damage.

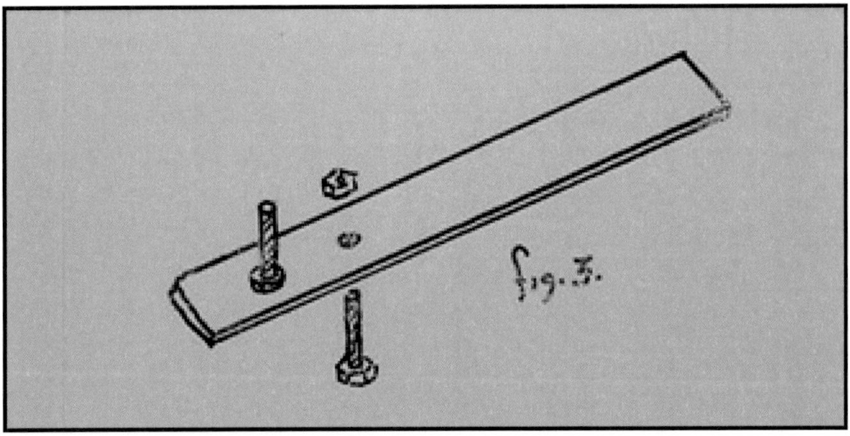

Figure three, this is a simple peg spanner made from strip steel to suit the piston end of a Dolla Mk II or Super Briton. Two or more holes are drilled in the strip to agree with the item to be undone, steel screws are inserted through the strip and secured with nuts on the opposite side, the screws should then be shortened to suit whatever is being undone. A simple modification of this tool made by filing the screw ends to a screwdriver tip will enable the rounded slotted nuts which have the bolt passing through the middle of the nut to be undone.

Basic repairs.

Most versions of gats consist of a barrel section containing the spring, barrel piston and washers and a grip section holding the trigger, sear and sear spring.

In order to repair a gat the first thing to check is to make sure its empty. With the gun un-cocked, remove the pellet pusher pin and look through the barrel, if blocked use a cleaning or clearing rod to remove any pellets or other blockage.

Once the gun is empty fit the muzzle nut into the wooden vice blocks and secure, try gently revolving the pistol to see if the nut unscrews, if it is tight lever back the spring and/or spring shroud and either wrap the stiff leather or clamp the clothes peg to the barrel then apply pliers or mole grips to them and rotate the barrel, the barrel nut should come loose easily and once it has undone about two threads hold the pistol by the grip and apply forward pressure to absorb any remaining spring tension while continuing to rotate the pistol until the barrel nut comes free. Remove the spring and any spring shroud before trying to remove the barrel and piston unit from the pistol.

To remove the piston/barrel unit, place the muzzle on a wood block and gently push down, remembering to keep the trigger pulled in order for the piston to clear the sear. Remove the barrel and check condition of washer which is either fitted at the far end of the cylinder or on the front of the piston block, replace washers as necessary, check barrel for straightness and clear the air transfer holes just in front of the piston block.

To obtain access to the grip section sears and trigger springs it is usually possible on Harrington Gats, Dolla's, tinplate Diana's and the clones to remove the grip screws and either the grip splits apart or in the case of tin-plates need to be pried apart to access the mechanism. However in the case of wooden grip pistols the grip can only be removed by knocking out the cross pins holding the grip which needs to be done very carefully to avoid knocking great chunks out of the grip surface. On this type of pistol the trigger and sear mechanisms may be in a sub frame welded to the cylinder with parts secured by cross pins, ensure that the pins are always refitted where they originated.

Typical layout of gat type pistol showing extreme simplicity of mechanism.

As can be seen above the layout is very simple and any faults can only be due to the sear spring breaking or being misplaced, the sear or its seating face wearing or the actual sear or trigger breaking.

Repairs.

To check sear engagement insert barrel back into the cylinder and see if it holds when the thumb is pressed hard on the rear of the piston, if it slips it may be due to either wear on the sear engagement surface which can be examined and if worn dressed back with an oilstone or diamond file or as is more likely the sear or trigger springs have weakened or broken, replace the offending article and repeat the thumb push test, the problem should now be resolved. The only other problem is usually the pellet pusher pin, sometimes they are lost and replaced with pushers from other pistols which may not be the correct length to push the pellets past the air transfer ports in the barrel, but the main problem seems to be loss of the sealing washer, these can easily be made using a drill and craft knife to fashion a washer from scrap leather.

Making a pellet pushing pin.

One of the most annoying faults is the loss of the pusher pin, sometimes these are or were available as spares or could be sourced from scrap pistols. Should none of these options be available, a good working replacement can be made using a nut and bolt from your scrap box (everyone should own a box of assorted bits and pieces that are too good to throw out). Choosing a bolt that suits the thread of the barrel, carefully drill a hole in the end of the bolt to take a suitable pusher rod, a broken 1/16th inch drill shank is ideal, ensure it is long enough to push the pellet past the air transfer ports. Run the nut up the bolt to a position where the depth of tread suits the tread in the barrel. Remove from pistol and either solder or superglue the pin and nut in position, fit a sealing washer under nut and the pusher is ready to use.

If you are lucky enough to own or have access to a lathe the nut and bolt head can be turned down to improve the appearance or a whole new pin could be made.

Re-assembly.

When refitting parts place a drop of good quality oil on pivot points, lubricate the washers also the sliding portion of the barrel, re-assembly is basically a reverse of the stripping operation, to refit the main spring is not a great problem, usually these springs are not particularly strong and if the barrel nut is fitted in the wooden vice blocks and is retained horizontally in the bench vice, body weight can be applied and the pistol rotated as the spring is compressed, the nut will soon engage and can be tightened in the same manner as when it was unscrewed. When the pistol is reassembled, stand it on its end with the pellet pusher in place and drop two or three drops of thin oil down the barrel, allow the pistol to stand for an hour or so. Before firing pellets pump the barrel back and forward a few times with the trigger pulled to circulate oil in the cylinder.

Notes.

There are some very useful exploded diagrams on pages 81 and 83 of the Diana SP50 section which show how the slightly more complex cylinder of this type of pistol is constructed, the only thing that is different is having to accurately line up the notch on the steel inner cylinder with the nose of the sear when reassembling the pistol.